TEACHING MATTERS

TEACHING AND LEARNING IN HIGHER EDUCATION
James M. Lang, Series Editor
Michelle D. Miller, Series Editor

A list of titles in this series appears at the end of this volume.

TEACHING MATTERS

A Guide for Graduate Students

Aeron Haynie and
Stephanie Spong

West Virginia University Press
Morgantown

First edition published 2022 by West Virginia University Press
Printed in the United States of America

ISBN 978-1-952271-54-0 (cloth) / 978-1-952271-55-7 (paperback) /
978-1-952271-56-4 (ebook)

Library of Congress Control Number:
2021053316

Cover design by Than Saffel / WVU Press

For Sophie Lyda and Ama Frances,
who teach us the most important things.

CONTENTS

ACKNOWLEDGMENTS

We dedicate this book first to our families: Thomas Heine, Roena Haynie-Reitz, Charles Reitz, Deirdre Haynie, Emile Haynie, the late Charles Haynie, Andrew McCollom, Edith Spong, Robert Spong, and Amy King. Aeron and Stephanie both work on an administrative schedule with limited time or leave for research and publication. This means that the vast majority of this book was written and revised in the evenings and on the weekends—while our families helped with dinner, childcare, feeding the cats, or walking the dog. We'd also like to thank our colleagues at the Center for Teaching and Learning from whom we have learned a tremendous amount about student learning and faculty development. Thanks to Kevin Gannon for his initial encouragement and to Chuck Paine for his helpful comments on our book proposal. Aeron wishes to thank the University of New Mexico Provost's office for supporting her research with some reassigned time over the summer. We also dedicate this book to the phenomenal current and former graduate students who agreed to be interviewed: Josefina Bittar, Kalila Bohsali, Benjamin Burnett, Kimberly Fournier, Erin Gould, Abdelbaset Haridy, Mary Hershberger, Motomi Kajitani, Jonathan Keller, Jairo Marshall, Emma Minks, David Paez, Kellen Paine, Stephanie M. Sanchez, Daniel Shattuck, Andrew Taylor, Margaret Wilkins, and Satya Wit. And, finally, a shout-out to all our former students at the

University of Florida, University of New Mexico, University of Montana-Western, University of Wisconsin-Green Bay, and Valencia College whose generosity and openness have made teaching a joy.

We'd like to acknowledge that our title, Teaching Matters, pays homage to Gail Mellow's work in *Taking College Seriously: Pedagogy Matters* (2015). Her volume highlighted the changing demographics of college students and the need for more reflective, collaborative teaching practices. We'd also like to acknowledge that Black Lives Matter has become a rallying cry for a world-wide racial justice movement. This book is intended neither to diminish the historically specific impact and meaning of that phrase nor to appropriate it unreflectively. We deeply believe that thoughtful, informed teaching can help diminish inequities in education; however, systematic, structural changes are needed for real justice.

CHAPTER 1

WHY TEACHING MATTERS

The first time Maria, a graduate student in anthropology, taught a class, the experience was so demoralizing that when it was over she no longer wanted to be a professor. She had been assigned the introductory course three weeks before the beginning of the semester. The only advice from the department chair had been to look at another instructor's syllabus. "No one talked to me about pedagogy, no one shared teaching or adult learning resources, and certainly no one taught me how to create a syllabus or structure the class toward specific learning outcomes." Each Tuesday evening she faced a class of 30 sleepy and apathetic undergraduates:

> I felt like I was being tortured and, worse yet, that I was torturing these students. My limited perspective at the time, based entirely on my experience as a student, was that my job was to stand in front of the classroom, an irregularly shaped pentagon that reflected my awkwardness, and fill students with necessary information. And so I diligently prepared outlines for long lectures that were occasionally interspersed with class discussions and old anthropology films. Even in our occasional class discussions, it was less discussion and more students

> haphazardly responding to my questions and prompts. There were moments when silence filled the room and then one of the more attentive and forgiving students would offer a thought or question to break the stillness. Even now, I am grateful for those students, all three of them, who rescued me so often in those dull, uninspired lectures. The students and I slogged through learning the basics about how humans organize and make sense of the world around them. Our collective and unspoken goal was simply to get through the semester. I felt incapable of teaching and completely lost in the classroom. I was stuck believing that teaching was a talent one either possesses or lacks, and I fell in the latter category. As someone who was struggling unawares with impostor syndrome, I internalized what I considered my inability to teach until it damaged my sense of self. At the time, I thought if I cannot teach the basic principles of anthropology, I have no business as a faculty member. Coupled with a tremendous sense that my department was unsupportive and not designed for someone like me (first-generation, working-class woman of color), I decided that academia was not where I belonged.

It was another two years before Maria began teaching again, but this time she had acquired new skills, honed other skills that had served her well, and was uplifted by both a supportive academic department and a professional setting that emphasized growth in teaching and learning. In each of these spaces, she started to feel that her experiences and background were assets in teaching and learning and that the practice of teaching was made visible as something that can be developed. Discussions about cultural aspects of learning, effective strategies in the classroom, and a higher purpose in teaching reflected back to her what she had always wanted higher education to be. "I realized I was not a terrible instructor after all. I just had never been taught how to teach."[1]

Teaching your first college class can be nerve-racking, even under the best of circumstances. After all, you're not yet an expert in the field, you may not be much older than the undergraduates in front of you, and you're juggling the new challenge of teaching along with the intense pressure of graduate studies. Although research universities are starting to take the teaching of undergraduates more seriously (Boyer, 1990; Patel, 2017), preparing and supporting graduate students' teaching practice is still not a priority in many departments. For graduate students like Maria, who are thrown into the classroom with no training or mentorship, teaching can be a demoralizing experience. Even graduate students lucky enough to receive some classroom training rarely learn about new advances in learning science or how to teach inclusively. Not every graduate student has a teaching mentor or a space in which they feel comfortable discussing problems that arise in teaching. We have designed this book to fill in these gaps and to be a helpful guide for graduate students who are beginning their journeys as college teachers. We hope that it will be useful for those graduate students who do not receive pedagogical training from their departments, and even for those who wish to supplement their disciplinary teaching courses with a more general resource. We believe now more than ever that teaching matters: it matters to you and your future success as a professor, and it matters to the students you teach.

As authors, we have 30 years of combined experience teaching at the college level—in both face-to-face (F2F) and online environments. We both have PhDs in literature and Aeron is an associate professor in the English Department and is an affiliated faculty member in the Department of

Organization, Information, and Learning Sciences at the University of New Mexico (UNM). After 20 years as a professor teaching British literature and interdisciplinary humanities courses, Aeron turned her attention to the scholarship of teaching and learning and has published on literary pedagogy and, more broadly, signature pedagogies. She is now executive director of the Center for Teaching and Learning at UNM where she also teaches pedagogy courses for graduate students. After graduate school, Stephanie went on to work as an instructional designer and then to direct a center for faculty development at a community college. Upon her return to UNM to direct the Center for Digital Learning, she also accepted an affiliated faculty role with the Department of Organization, Information, and Learning Sciences where she supports undergraduates and graduate students in learning design, faculty development, and distance education projects. Between the two of us, we've worked at research intensive, regional comprehensive, small liberal arts, and community colleges. We now work with faculty and graduate teaching assistants across many disciplines in F2F, hybrid, and online environments. At UNM, a research-intensive (R1) Hispanic-serving institution (HSI) with a large number of first-generation students, we are fortunate to work with and learn from a group of faculty, staff, and administrators committed to supporting a diverse student body.[2]

Over the years we've fielded many questions from new graduate student instructors about how best to establish their teaching practice. When we were graduate students, we were told to put teaching last and to focus on our research. And it's true that teaching has the potential to take up an incredible amount of your time and thus inhibit your progress toward finishing your degree. Yet we have a responsibility to our students who need to learn the skills and material we are teaching if they are going to succeed in college. We became fascinated by the contrast between classes that inspired and transformed students and those that bored or discouraged them. Teaching, for us, became a serious intellectual puzzle that we began researching and discussing even as we continued to research our primary disciplinary areas. How could we transmit to undergraduate students our own passion for our subjects? How could we design a course so that students were engaged and motivated, instead of passive and bored? Although as instructors we are not solely responsible for a student's success or failure, we observed that some professors consistently inspire their students. We wanted to know more about how to create these types of learning experiences. What we found is that contrary to popular misconceptions, good teaching is not an innate personality trait, nor does it always result from subject matter expertise.

If someone has a graduate degree in a field of study, it is assumed that they can teach this subject at the college level. College instructors are not required to take courses in pedagogy or to be familiar with current research on how people learn. To put it another way, if we approached scholarship the way we have historically approached college teaching, we would ask budding scholars to read little about their fields and hope that their solitary, naïve efforts would miraculously result in brilliant research discoveries. Just as this untrained approach would not result in sound research, neither does it result in good teaching. Of course there will be exceptions, folks who somehow manage to become inspiring teachers despite a lack of training or engagement in current learning science research. However, this model puts an enormous amount of pressure on graduate students to somehow intuitively blossom into skilled teachers, and it disproportionally rewards charisma. It also offers little support for those who initially struggle.

It might be surprising to learn that there is a growing body of research on higher education pedagogy. For example, there have been many studies on whether "active learning" increases students' understanding of math and science (Freeman et al., 2014), how an instructor's own attitudes about intelligence (whether it's "fixed" or can grow) impacts the success of minoritized students in math and science courses (Canning et al., 2019), the benefits of group work (Cooper, 2000), how reflective writing can increase student motivation (Schippers et al., 2015), what types of undergraduate study habits are more productive (Brown et al., 2014), and which specific feedback can help reduce feelings of "imposter syndrome" in students (Yaeger et al., 2013). Not all these studies will be pertinent to your own teaching practice, but some may profoundly change how you think about teaching and learning and what you choose to do in the classroom. Some research may reaffirm what you're already doing while others may cause you to radically revamp a teaching practice. For example, as someone who teaches writing-intensive courses, Aeron routinely begins her classes with short, timed freewrites. It was an intuitive decision aimed to help students collect their thoughts about the day's assigned reading. Research shows that this is an effective way to promote active learning in many disciplines (Nevid, Pastva, & Mcclelland, 2012; Angelo & Cross, 1993). On the other hand, Aeron found out that the detailed comments and corrections that she laboriously made on her students' papers are not an effective (or efficient) way to help students learn to write better (Haswell, 1983). This was a counterintuitive discovery, but a very useful one! This book summarizes the most impactful research and also points you toward places where you can read more. Throughout this book we encourage you to develop your own unique teaching practice that fits your personality, is appropriate for the goals of your discipline, and is grounded in research.

While we encourage you to learn from the research on teaching and learning, actual teaching will always provide surprises and challenges. That is because teaching is an intensely human, personal experience. You are building a relationship with your students, asking them to trust your knowledge of the subject, your fairness, and your commitment to their success. In addition, you are working in an environment that is based on a decidedly Anglo-American upper/upper middle-class tradition that can marginalize students from other races, cultures, and socioeconomic classes. To be an effective instructor means recognizing that it will take work to ensure that all your students feel a sense of belonging in your classroom. That feeling of belonging is essential: a student's experience in your class might inspire them to major in your field or may provide them with their only experience looking at the world from the perspective of your discipline.

Even when we begin a course with the best of intentions and plans, there will be times when our students' behavior will baffle us. For example, once a student fell asleep in the first row of Aeron's class and began snoring loudly to the amusement of other students.[3] Students fail to turn in final assignments, show up without having read the material, and sometimes act in ways that are inexplicable to you. In the absence of information, we will make assumptions: that some students are unmotivated, disrespectful, or even that they are incapable of doing college-level work. After all, we may reason, we would have never done this when we were in college! It helps to remember, however, that most graduate students have had a unique experience with secondary and undergraduate education. Most likely you were at the top of your college class and you thrived in the educational systems you encountered. You may have had close relationships with professors who valued your ideas and the contribution you could make to your field. Maybe you had parents who supported your academic success and who modelled academic excellence. If you are a member of a privileged group—white, middle class, upper class, able bodied, cisgendered, have college-educated parents, a legal citizen, etc.—then you may not recognize the ways that our educational system has created barriers to some students' success or the challenges they have already overcome just to be in college. We often assume students will learn the way we learned and that they can be taught the way that we were taught. Chapters 4 and 5 will give you strategies to learn more about your students so that you don't have to rely on unfounded assumptions.

Just as it's tempting to teach the way you were taught, your graduate professors may be preparing you for the research jobs they have, jobs that don't necessarily emphasize teaching. If they advise you to place research first, they are giving you the strategies that worked well for them. However, most graduate students will not follow that path. According to the *Digest of Educational Statistics*, less than one-third of those instructors who have secured full-time positions work at research universities. Many fields in the humanities, such as history, are facing record low numbers of tenure track positions and fewer than 20% of those positions are at R1 institutions (Kang, n.d.).[4] Whereas it may be your goal to become a professor at a research university, most full-time academic positions are ones that value sound teaching—in different ways and with different corresponding research expectations. For example, positions at select small liberal arts colleges expect active research agendas, good teaching, and student advisement and mentoring. Regional comprehensives are similar but may allow some latitude in where and what one publishes. Community colleges have heavy teaching loads and don't require publications, though some community college teachers publish, nonetheless. Research universities, too, are becoming increasingly concerned with undergraduate retention and graduation rates, which are significantly impacted by the quality of undergraduate teaching. The mode of your teaching may also be quite different than your graduate professors have experienced. Even before the 2020–2021 COVID-19 health crisis, colleges and universities were very interested in growing ranks of online faculty who could develop flexible programs to increase enrollment without incurring the additional cost of expanding physical classroom spaces. However "older and higher-ranking faculty" have reported the greatest *disinterest* in teaching online (Ubell, 2017, p. 52). Online and hybrid enrollments have increased each year and about a third of all students (pre-2020) have taken one online course (Seaman et al., 2018). However the current global health crisis resolves, online teaching will remain an increasingly important part of higher education. Teaching may also be where you find the greatest professional satisfaction. In a survey of more than 1,000 tenured and nontenured faculty across institutional types, the aspect of the job that garnered the most satisfied responses was "teaching students" at 91% with a close second in "mentoring students or junior faculty" at 87%; "conducting research" came in at only 68% (Anft, 2018, p. 6).

There is good reason to take satisfaction in teaching: few careers allow you to spend a significant part of your day introducing others to a subject that you love. Your ability to communicate your passion for your subject may change the direction of your students' careers, their lives, and their understanding of the world. Graduate students often teach introductory courses that determine an undergraduate student's future success in college. Some studies suggest that undergraduates may even be more likely to adopt a major when their initial coursework is led by a graduate student rather than a faculty member (Bettinger et al., 2016). Although you can't take sole responsibility for a student's success or failure, you want to know that you've done what you can to design your course and teach in a way that allows every student a chance for success. If you are teaching non-majors as part of a general education requirement, wouldn't you like them to at least have a basic understanding and appreciation of your discipline? After all, even if these students don't become majors, they will be voters, neighbors, and members of our communities. We'll talk more in Chapter 3 about ways to design your course to pivot around big ideas and key questions. These course design strategies will help you create a powerful learning experience for students as well as help you form your class into an active learning community.

The stakes are high for students attempting college in this historical moment. One in three students will not graduate in six years, and even fewer graduate in four (National Center for Education Statistics, 2018). College students now pay the highest costs for their educations and are generally in the most precarious financial circumstances.[5] There is a growing body of research that suggests students' early academic success provides momentum for graduation (Attewell et al., 2012; Jenkins & Bailey, 2017). None of this argues that front-door courses need to be made *easier*—since such a shift would not strengthen students' later success in college—but it does mean that we owe students our best efforts. We are not exaggerating when we say that you may have a larger impact than you may believe. Since the 1980s, there has been a consensus that the relationship between students and their instructors has an astonishing impact on student motivation and engagement (Chickering & Gamson, 1987). As institutions have become more interested in how higher education improves the living conditions of citizens, we've seen an even richer portrait of the impact individual instructors can make. A survey of more than 30,000 college graduates, conducted by the Gallup organization and Purdue University, found that when it comes to a college degree translating to "a good life," the experiences college students have matter much more than where they went to college—and this holds true across public, private, small, and large institutions. "If graduates had a professor who cared about them as a person, made them excited about learning, and encouraged them to pursue their dreams, their odds of being engaged at work more than doubled, as did their odds of thriving in their well-being" (Gallup, 2014, p. 4). The dark side of these results is that only 14% of graduates strongly agreed that they had those experiences (Gallup, 2014). We can all relate to the need to be recognized or seen, and we know that small gestures from someone else may have a large impact on us personally. This is especially true when you are new to college. When Stephanie was a first-semester freshman, one of her professors gave two grades on every paper: one for ideas and one for writing. Although Stephanie was a beginning writer at the college level, having her professor engage sincerely with her ideas made her feel recognized and gave her a sense of the potential that could come with more practice on her writing. When Aeron began her first week of college, a professor remembered her name from their brief chat at registration. This simple act helped Aeron feel like she had a place in the class and at the university. There are countless small moments where our attention can make students feel seen, valued, and encouraged.

Teaching with Compassion and Flexibility

The experience of today's college students has been impacted by the COVID-19 pandemic, which raised philosophical questions about the value of higher education. Must students be on a physical campus in order to have a real college experience? What does it mean to create classroom community? How can we design our courses to accommodate students' health and living conditions? And while these questions are a product of a unique historical moment, this is also what it means to teach in every moment. In our conversations with instructors, we encourage them to respond to students with compassion and flexibility. We ask them to structure their courses to allow all students to succeed despite their complicated, often fraught lives. Even in non-pandemic times, college students face illness, anxiety, economic uncertainty, poverty, uneven access to WIFI, caretaking burdens, and other real-life constraints. You will be prepared to help students who face challenges or through transition times if you develop compassionate and flexible strategies from the start.

Insights from Culturally Responsive Teaching and Learner-Centered Teaching

The demographics of college students have changed and instructors can no longer assume a student population of white, middle-class, native English speakers who live in the dorms and graduate in four years.[6] Teaching with compassion and flexibility means believing that, given the right conditions, all students can learn (Brookfield, 2015). One of the principles informing this book is the practice of *culturally responsive teaching* (CRT). Briefly, culturally responsive teaching recognizes that minoritized students' cultures are often excluded in the academy and that their life experiences are often treated as deficits; however, when students' culture and experiences are leveraged appropriately they can strengthen and deepen students' learning (Gay, 2000; Ladson-Billings, 1995; Ginsberg & Wlodkowski, 2015; Hammond, 2015; Chávez and Longerbeam, 2016.[7]) CRT asks us to give students opportunities to use their own cultural assets in our courses and encourages us to make the tacit assumptions of our courses (the *hidden curriculum*) more explicit. It can be daunting to imagine how you might respond to all the cultures represented in your classroom, but CRT only asks you to assume that you will have students whose cultural habits and backgrounds don't match your own. What might it mean to create flexible learning environments that intentionally support students' cultural strengths? In Chapter 2 we'll help you build more structured and transparent course designs to make your own hidden curriculum explicit to students; in Chapter 3 we'll discuss how to create a welcoming classroom community, and in Chapter 4 we'll help you to plan classes that employ more active learning and intentional discussions in which all students participate.

All these strategies are grounded in the principles of learner-centered teaching, which guides most effective and evidenced-based teaching strategies. A learner-centered approach to teaching is based on the educational theory of constructivism[8] that shifts the focus of teaching from the teacher to the students. One way to think of it is that in a learner-centered class, success is measured by the brilliance of the students, not the brilliance of the instructor. To be learner-centered doesn't mean that students have all the power in the classroom or that the course is designed around their likes and dislikes. Learner-centered means designing your course so students have opportunities to practice the skills you demonstrate, and it involves giving students some responsibility and choice in the classroom.

What You Will Find in This Book

This book is meant to support you as you develop your own teaching practice, to give you access to exciting new developments in learning sciences, and to invite you to engage in the larger questions concerning higher education. We will also share practical tips and techniques that have proven successful for other teachers and we will help prepare you for your first academic teaching job. However, we know that each of you will have different assumptions about education and varied goals for yourselves as teachers, and that you will develop unique teaching personas. This book is designed to help you begin your own pedagogical practice on sound footing, to support you, and to encourage you to seek out teaching collaborators—in print, through virtual communities, or in real life.

Each of the following chapters begins by asking large, conceptual questions, then provides theoretical grounding, includes evidence-based applications, and explains the differences in applying the techniques in F2F, hybrid, and online teaching. In Chapter 2 we discuss how you can best design your course to facilitate deep, lasting learning. Although we realize that not all graduate students are able to design their own courses, it's still useful to think hard about the most important skills/understandings you want students to take away from your course. In Chapter 3 we consider how you build a classroom learning community in which all students feel empowered to succeed. Chapter 4 suggests ways to plan your classes to increase students' opportunities for active learning and engaged participation. Chapter 5 addresses common challenges in the classroom and gives strategies for anticipating and responding to them. In Chapter 6 we outline how to create meaningful assignments and respond to student work. Chapter 7 includes interviews with graduate students that highlight common challenges new instructors face and offers a variety of ways to prepare and respond. In Chapter 8, we close the book with a call for you to care for yourself as a graduate student so that you can sustain your teaching practice. There are also three Appendices that you'll find useful: Appendix 1 (Help! What if My Course Starts Next Week?) provides a just-in-time guide for when you need quick advice; Appendix 2 takes you through the steps to draft a strong teaching statement for academic job applications and outlines how best to prepare for an on-campus teaching demonstration; and Appendix 3 offers you a list of topical resources to continue your own learning about learning.

In the end, no matter how many techniques, theories, and practices you learn (and we hope that you will learn many), teaching will always be an unpredictable endeavor. What works with one class might not work with the next. The dynamics of the classroom change with the students, the fluctuating rhythms of the academic calendar, the political climate, and community health crises. This is why it is important to develop a scholarly and reflective approach to your teaching. One book cannot transform you from novice to expert teacher, but the following chapters will give you a strong foundation on which to build your practice. Our goal is to help you feel more prepared and thus more confident in approaching your teaching so that you can better serve your students.

CHAPTER 2

HOW DO YOU DESIGN A COURSE?

Have you ever sat in a class as a student and wondered *Why are we doing this?* or *How will this be useful to me?* Like you, your students have limited time, bandwidth, and attention to give to your course. They will be more motivated if they know the purpose behind each component of your course and how those components will support their future goals. As you read this book, you also might be designing your own strategy for completing your coursework, exams, writing, presenting, and publication so that you have the right skills and experiences to graduate.[1] You might be planning how to turn seminar papers into dissertation chapters, which conferences you need to present at, or which labs you want to be a part of so that you can land a job after graduate school. This strategizing is just one example of how you already use a method known as *backward design*: you have a goal and you are carefully identifying and organizing the steps you will need to take to reach that goal.

In teaching, backward design is planning your courses with the end in mind; the *end* is not what content you want to cover but *how you want your students to be changed.* What goals do you want students to accomplish? What skills or knowledge should they acquire? What concepts should they understand by the time they complete the course? What big ideas or frameworks do you want them to be able to use five years after they have completed your course? These questions are purposefully capacious and challenging, and you may find yourself refining your answers after each semester you teach a course. Not all of you will be teaching courses that you design from scratch. It will still be valuable for you to have a clear understanding of what students should get out of a course so that you can communicate it to your students.

In this book, we are going to encourage you to think of backward design in three layers. First, we want you focus on the big picture, the ideas or skills that you want students to take away from your course (Wiggens & McTighe, 2005). Second, we want you to design learning experiences that will provide students with authentic and engaging opportunities to build their knowledge and skills. Lastly, we want you to design a welcoming environment that helps students know that they belong and that they can meaningfully make progress in your course through both their achievements and their mistakes. Each of these facets of backward design are important to creating a cohesive and inclusive learning experience for your students.

When we start teaching, many of us are handed a textbook or set of materials to cover rather than encouraged to engage in big-picture thinking. If our textbook has 15 chapters and our semester has 15 weeks, shazam, we're set! This is often referred to as the coverage model, and it haunts all disciplines despite longstanding research that more material does not equate to more learning. Think about the courses you've taken where coverage was the goal and the instructor was hell-bent on making it through all 22 chapters regardless of students' exasperation or the instructor's own inability to make all the content relevant. As a student in a class like this, you might have felt overwhelmed by the material. You might have also felt frustrated by the amount of work you did to keep up with the content and deflated if a few assessments covered only part of the content but accounted for the sum of your grade. What do you still remember from courses like this? Likely, not much.

We are teaching at a time when much of our course content is already available to students for free somewhere (in the library, online, from massive open online courses or MOOCs, etc.), so if we aren't designing for their learning then we may quickly find ourselves irrelevant. Another way to think of it is, if you don't want students to treat your course like a box they have to check before they graduate, then don't treat your course like a series of boxes they have to check. Just as you are designing your own professional success, design your course with careful thought about its context and the learning goals you hope students achieve once they have completed the term. Courses predicated on coverage are hard to manage for both faculty and students as they try to sort through the excess to make meaning out of the material. Robin Smith (2014) drives this point home with the following thought experiment:

> What if you knew your learners were going to be tested six months from now and you would be compensated based on their retention of your course content? How would you teach differently?
>
> - Would you reduce the amount of material you cover?
> - Would you make sure you don't overload the learners with extraneous information?

- Would you give information in a format compatible with their learning [preferences]?
- Would you ask them what format is the most helpful to their learning?
- Would you not care how they received the information, so long as they learned it?
- Would you provide practice opportunities?

Smith reminds us that just because you've covered it, doesn't mean that students have learned it. If real, lasting student learning is our goal, what teaching practices are most helpful in achieving it?

Grant Wiggins and Jay McTighe (2005) outline backward design, or what they call "understanding by design," in three stages: (1) identify what deep learning and skills you want students to have achieved at the end of the course; (2) determine what you would accept as proof that students have achieved those results; and (3) plan their learning experiences and your instruction so that students can demonstrate their progress. Once you know what it is that you hope students will learn and how you'll know they've learned it, *scaffolding* is the process of building smaller chunks of knowledge and skills to help students produce evidence that the larger learning goal has been achieved. And *assessments* are the key moments or benchmarks where you test the effectiveness of your teaching by asking students to produce something that allows you to measure how well they are learning. These benchmarks could be very simple, such as asking students to solve a problem in class or more substantial assignments like a quiz, presentation, or exam. (Assessments don't always have to be graded assignments: we will get to that in Chapters 4 and 6.)

Backward design allows us to map out a plan for success

for our students, and to map out a plan for our own success as educators. This should give you some relief as a new instructor. There are lots of great strategies out there to improve your teaching (we have tried to capture the most impactful ones in this book), but strategies alone will never be as useful to you as your own process of articulating your learning goals, scaffolding the steps to meet those goals, assessing student progress toward those goals, and reflecting on the effectiveness of your efforts. John Biggs (1999) reminds us that effective teaching is always dependent on our ability to observe and reflect on exactly what we are doing as educators. "There is no single, all-purpose best method of teaching," he argues, "It depends on how we *conceive* the process of teaching, and through reflection come to some conclusion about how we may do our particular job better." What's most important is that you develop a practice of careful planning, examining evidence of student learning, reflecting on your teaching, and redesigning your courses.

Learner-Centered Course Design

Backward design starts with articulating for yourself the unique skills and deep learning your course will help students develop. This process ensures that you are teaching "through the lens of learning, rather than focusing on teaching and letting the students learn where they can" (Lang 2008). This is called *learner-centered teaching,* or the idea that learning is the most important thing that happens in a classroom. Our goals, planning efforts, and the measure of our course's effectiveness should focus on the learning we want to occur in the students and to what extent it does occur. As an illustration, when Stephanie teaches a yoga class, she could simply go through the sequence herself and only demonstrate the moves for students. And, while the students might watch her attentively and the movements might be very polished, students wouldn't actually learn much. Instead, they need to practice the movements themselves. Even if they are initially clumsy or imperfect, students will learn much more from this practice than simply observing Stephanie. Practicing the movements requires more effort on the students' part and asks them to be more vulnerable. If someone walked into the class, the students' poses might look messier than a single expert performing each move. This strategy requires Stephanie to let students make decisions about how they are going to practice the movements, when to take breaks, and what modifications to use. Instead of being easier on the instructor, this learner-centered approach requires more effort on her part; she must clearly guide students with a variety of abilities through the movements they are practicing, circulate around the room to notice where students are, and give feedback so that they can all strengthen their muscles and build flexibility. We want students to take their learning with them when they leave our courses and use it to become more independent, lifelong learners.

At this point you may be thinking, "yes, but this was not the way that I learned!" And, you are probably right. We both can think of numerous classes from our undergraduate degrees where lots of material was covered but where we did not gain a big picture or set of key takeaways for understanding that discipline. Even a course that seems to be based on process can fall victim to the coverage model. For example, in her first semester of teaching, Stephanie was handed a prepackaged unit on report writing for her freshman writing course. It was a huge relief to have materials created for her since she was only introduced to the course she would be teaching a week before the term started, and she dutifully taught the materials to students and graded their assignments. She taught the coverage model: do these things, in this order, with the aim of having students read all the materials and produce a final project. The report was one in a whole list of genres she could teach in this freshman writing course, but she never really had a sense of how it was going to support her students in their other writing intensive courses, or how it would impact their understanding of research or working with primary sources. The unit wasn't a disaster, but when she received subpar assignments and challenges on a few student grades, it was tedious and taxing. All told, it seemed similar to most of the courses she had taken as an undergraduate—but she didn't have a clear understanding of what (or, even if) students were learning.

While Stephanie was teaching this unit, she was simultaneously developing the rest of the course. In a practicum, she was asked to lay out her units with learning outcomes, identify the knowledge and skills a student would need to have to be successful in the unit projects, and create smaller assignments that helped students develop the necessary knowledge and skills. Here, she was putting backward design into practice. It allowed her to think critically about what success looked like in her course and what a student would need to know and do to be able to demonstrate their learning. Once her course moved into the units that she had designed herself with backward design, assignments became easier to grade and there were far fewer challenges to student grades. In large part, backward design gave Stephanie and the students a better sense of the purpose of the course and their pathway to reaching those learning goals. Looking back, she realized she could have helped her students in that first unit by thinking about the prepared material in the same way she later thought about the material she designed. Many of us are given prepared materials, but we can better support students' learning by questioning the thinking behind that prescribed material to better translate it for students.

Without backward design, instructors are challenged to describe what learning actually takes place in our classrooms, or how to determine if students are achieving any benefit from spending a semester in our course. For example, in a beginning economics course, students will likely read about the concept of supply and demand. However, what are students able to do with that information? Can they analyze the 2020 news accounts of toilet paper shortages to explain how supply and demand is affecting their lives? Our specific goals for students' learning are often called *learning outcomes*. A learning outcome for the above economics course might be "students will be able to apply the concept of supply and demand to current events." As educators we tend to think of the results of learning as boundless. While this is true, learning outcomes are a way to articulate our top priorities for student learning and explain these goals to our students. In their summary of research from the 1970s forward, Aaron Richmond et al. (2016) find that "more learning occurred when students had objectives than when they simply reviewed material without objectives." Backward design asks you to start with your learning outcomes and build your course around those end goals.

As a graduate instructor, you have probably been provided the learning outcomes for the course you will be teaching, which can be very helpful. It gives you more time to think about how to make these learning outcomes clear to students and how the assignments they are asked to complete are connected to those outcomes. In the next section we're going to help you unpack learning outcomes that you didn't write. It's entirely possible you might encounter learning outcomes that are either poorly written or unwelcoming to students no matter how generously you analyze them. Poorly written learning outcomes often fall into two categories: they are too general or are they are not written in student-friendly language. Overly general or vague outcomes are those than can't be measured, such as "in taking this course students will *learn* the political, social, economic, and cultural history of Europe from the 1600s to the present time." This is more of a description of *what the course will cover* than it is a statement about what students will have gained. How would we measure students learning? Is there a gauge inside their heads that moves as they gain new knowledge? Another common mistake is to describe learning goals in terms of what students will become familiar with; for example, "in this art history course, students will become familiar with the major movements in art from baroque to modern." More measurable outcomes are those that state what students should be able to do, such as in the following outcome from Delta College: "Upon successful completion of this course, the student will be able to compose an effective narrative that analyzes the history of later Western civilization in response to an analytical question" (2021). This outcome tells us what the student will do: *compose* a narrative and *analyze* an aspect of Western civilization. It's still not a particularly engaging outcome. It may be that you are teaching a course with prescribed outcomes that aren't written in engaging, student-friendly language. If this is the case, use this next section to help you rewrite those outcomes *in your own words for the benefit of your students*. No one wins if you and your students think your course outcomes are worthless, so don't be afraid to revise them for everyone's benefit.

Working with What You've Got

You have options to make learning outcomes meaningful for your students, regardless of who wrote them. You might leave the official outcomes you've been given on your syllabus and then add a paragraph where you translate them into more accessible language. You could also work with your students collectively to revise them during the first week, or you might have students draft individualized goals for learning in the first week and then have them reflect on those goals throughout the course. For example, consider this not particularly accessible outcome for an introduction to sociology course at Northern Arizona University:

> [In this course students will] apply basic concepts, such as culture, social change, socialization, stratification, social structure, institutions, and differentiations (e.g., race/ethnicity, class, gender, sexuality) and their theoretical interrelations to analyze social trends, conflicts, reciprocal relationships between individuals and society, and social policies. (Luna, 2018)

This outcome might not mean much to a student new to the study of sociology. Compare it to this more accessible language from Randolf College: "[Students will] understand the 'relative' nature of the world in which we live and how using the 'sociological imagination' can help us see our life and the world around us in new and more critical ways" (Currier, 2020).

Most of us begin our teaching careers working with predetermined learning outcomes, and this can be a great opportunity to learn something about the pedagogy of your discipline. Do your outcomes represent new thoughts or important challenges your discipline positions itself to address?

Do they assume social or historical contexts? What kinds of paradigms of value or knowledge making do they presume? Do they answer to particular disciplinary associations or accrediting boards? Analyzing your prescribed outcomes now will also better prepare you to develop course or program outcomes later when afforded the opportunity to develop them from scratch. Being able to unpack these nuances efficiently for first-year college students and nonmajors will also prepare you to talk about your discipline and research to nonexperts, whether this be in a hiring committee or in a grant application. If your learning outcomes aren't immediately clear for first-year students or nonmajors, but they make sense to you, take it as a challenge to translate them to your students. Being able to explain and translate relevance is a skill that will serve you throughout your career, in academia or outside of it.

You can start by analyzing the parts of your learning outcomes. In its most basic construction, a student learning outcome should contain two parts, a verb and a noun: "the verb generally describes the intended *cognitive process*, and the noun generally describes the *knowledge* students are expected to acquire or construct" (Anderson and Krathwohl, 2000). For example, "Students will be able to construct a close reading of a literary passage." The verb here, *construct*, is the cognitive process we want students to be able to demonstrate; the noun here is *close reading*, the disciplinary step that we want students to understand. It's useful to think about these two parts of an outcome within the range of learning and cognitive processes we want students to experience. Educational theorist Benjamin Bloom developed a classification system to help describe the levels of cognition and knowledge that interplay in learning. An easy way to understand this taxonomy is in the matrix in Table 1, where

Table 1 Adapted Bloom's Table from ISU CELT

		Knowledge Dimension			
		Factual The basic elements a student must know to be acquainted with a discipline or solve problems in it.	*Conceptual* The interrelationships among the basic elements within a larger structure that enable them to function together.	*Procedural* How to do something, methods of inquiry, and criteria for using skills, algorithms, techniques, and methods.	*Metacognitive* Knowledge of cognition in general as well as awareness and knowledge of one's own cognition.
Cognitive Dimension	Remember Retrieve relevant knowledge from long-term memory.	*Remember + Factual* **List** primary and secondary colors.	*Remember + Conceptual* **Recognize** symptoms of exhaustion.	*Remember + Procedural* **Recall** how to perform CPR.	*Remember + Metacognitive* **Identify** strategies for retaining information.
	Understand Construct meaning from instructional messages, including oral, written and graphic communication.	*Understand + Factual* **Summarize** features of a new product.	*Understand + Conceptual* **Classify** adhesives by toxicity.	*Understand + Procedural* **Clarify** assembly instructions.	*Understand + Metacognitive* **Predict** one's response to culture shock.
	Apply Carry out or use a procedure in a given situation.	*Apply + Factual* **Respond** to frequently asked questions.	*Apply + Conceptual* **Provide** advice to novices.	*Apply + Procedural* **Carry out** pH tests of water samples.	*Apply + Metacognitive* **Use** techniques that match one's strengths.
	Analyze Carry out or use a procedure in a given situation.	*Analyze + Factual* **Select** the most complete list of activities.	*Analyze + Conceptual* **Differentiate** high and low culture.	*Analyze + Procedural* **Integrate** compliance with regulations.	*Analyze + Metacognitive* **Deconstruct** one's biases.

Table 1 (continued)

Knowledge Dimension				
Evaluate Make judgments based on criteria and standards.	*Evaluate + Factual* **Select** the most complete list of activities.	*Evaluate + Conceptual* **Determine** relevance of results.	*Evaluate + Procedural* **Judge** efficiency of sampling techniques.	*Evaluate + Metacognitive* **Reflect** on one's progress.
Create Put elements together to form a coherent whole; reorganize into a new pattern or structure.	*Create + Factual* **Generate** a log of daily activities.	*Create + Conceptual* **Assemble** a team of experts.	*Create + Procedural* **Design** efficient project workflow.	*Create + Metacognitive* **Create** a learning portfolio.

Note. A Model of Learning Objectives–based on *A Taxonomy for Learning, Teaching, and Assessing: A Revision of Bloom's Taxonomy of Educational Objectives*, by Rex Heer, Center for Excellence in Learning and Teaching, Iowa State University. Licensed under a Creative Commons Attribution-ShareAlike 4.0 International License.

levels of cognition and knowledge overlap from simple to more complex.

Classification systems like this can help you better understand how to orient your students to your learning outcomes, and they can also help you better understand how to scaffold or help students build toward those goals. For example, what smaller skills would a student need to know in order to construct a close reading? What do they need to know about their reading strategies, and what do they need to know about writing organization? Some disciplines have more prescribed outcomes than others. In STEM (science, technology, engineering, and mathematics) fields, there may be a set of formulas or strategies that must be mastered before a student can tackle progressively more advanced applications. For example, below are outcomes from an introductory-level physics course:

> At the end of this course you will be able to ***analyze*** physical systems (accelerating cars, orbiting planets, bridges, etc.) using two paradigms: (1) Newton's laws, and (2) conservation laws. You will be able to ***explain*** the effects of forces qualitatively. You will be able to ***draw predictions*** about physical systems as a result of calculations. (adapted from Dubson, n.d.)

Notice how the outcomes build on one another to demonstrate how they are interrelated. Students will use Newton's laws and conservation laws to first analyze examples of force in the world and explain the effects of force, then they will use that knowledge and those skills to make predictions about new physical systems.

Learning outcomes can also be an expression of larger goals, "essential questions" or "understandings" of a discipline or program (Wiggens & McTighe, 2005; Driscoll & Wood, 2007). These are not always agreed upon facts but demonstrate conversations in which a discipline continues to engage. For example, the following outcomes come from a 200-level American history survey (Creasman, 2016):

> Students will be able to
>
> 1. recall the principal persons, places, and events from the chronological framework of this course;
> 2. synthesize the thematic historical influences that shaped the modern history of the United States;
> 3. explain the impact of the individual, regardless of societal rank, as participants in the making of history;

4. assess the role that diversity plays in the shaping of the modern history of the United States;
5. detect the lessons, patterns or characteristics from historical events to better understand present day happenings;
6. interpret historical events by using appropriate historical methods;
7. demonstrate competency in civics literacy.

Looking at these outcomes, you can see central themes around the individual, diversity, and historical methods. The faculty teaching this course have positioned their subject as one with particular "methods" of sense making, but they haven't provided anything as clear cut as Newton's second law. These outcomes also assume that students will gain value from understanding the past, and the "lessons" they learn will help them better navigate or understand their present contexts. If we dig deeper, the outcomes also illustrate a tension between the role of the individual and the role of groups in affecting the course of historical events. All of this tells us something about how the instructors teaching this course think about the scope of American history, what pedagogical approaches they might use, or what they hope students will gain from the course.

Based on the verbs at the beginning of each outcome, we might even guess the kinds of assignments students will be asked to do. Outcomes can help you focus and limit what kinds of assignments will make sense for the learning you hope students achieve. While multiple-choice or identification questions would demonstrate student learning for the history course's first outcome, class discussions, written or presented analyses, live or video interpretations, or essay exams would be required for outcomes 3 through 6.

Outcome 7 reflects a recent state-mandated change requiring civic literacy to be a part of general education requirements, which we would only recognize by understanding the context in which these outcomes have been drafted. In Dubson's physics course above, problem sets, case studies, exams, and labs could all be used to meet outcomes focused on problem solving. For the outcome, "You will be able to explain the effects of forces qualitatively," it would be difficult to meet the goal through a multiple-choice test or quiz. However, students could demonstrate this outcome with written work or presentations. Implicit in the verb "explain" is a communication to someone. The instructor might even think creatively about how students should be able to explain their understanding to an expert audience using the class's vocabulary. Or, they could ask students to explain the effects in simplified terms for a nonexpert audience; in this instance, the instructor could ask students to use their own words to explain the effects of forces for a young cousin or grandparent unfamiliar with physics.

MORE DISCIPLINARY OUTCOMES TO CONSIDER

Geology: Students will be able to communicate geological concepts to peers and the public in both oral and written formats.

Psychology: Students will be able to identify appropriate basic research methods to test hypotheses empirically.

African American Studies: Students will be able to explain the significance of key individuals and events that shaped the culture and history of people of African descent in the U.S. and wider diaspora.

Mathematics: Students will be able to construct a mathematical proof.

Philosophy: Students will be able to evaluate normative standards governing social relations and practices through the lens of philosopher thinkers.

Accounting: Students will be able to execute effective research related to accounting.

Latin American Studies: Students will be able to identify textual ideologies from different historical moments, languages, and power structures.

Economics: Students will be able to accurately use quantitative methods from economic theory.

Outcomes adapted from Student Learning Outcomes by College/Program. (n.d.). *Assessment and Institutional Effectiveness*. Retrieved June 5, 2021, from https://www.fullerton.edu/data/assessment/assessment_at_csuf/outcomes.php

Learning outcomes are an opportunity to clarify your priorities for student learning and decide what to include in your course. They should help you focus your teaching when you have so many choices. It's one thing to write outcomes that say "Synthesize historical primary texts for thematic historical influences," and another to imagine what that would mean to you as a freshman or how meaningful you would find this outcome if you were a nonmajor. What do you do, in your field, when synthesizing something? What steps do you take, what kinds of information do you use, and how do you determine confluence or contradiction? How will you model that for your students? For each of your course outcomes, put pressure on the language and start to ask yourself these clarifying questions. You might consider arranging the learning outcomes for your course progressively, from foundational to more complex, to help you think about how the outcomes themselves build on one another, like the way Dubson's physics' outcomes above build upon each other. You could also write your outcomes in a narrative paragraph the way that the physics course is framed above. If you are still feeling uncertain about your prescribed learning outcomes, you might try rewriting them based on how you want students to incorporate their learning into their lives after your course. Dee Fink's (2013) list of generalized goals for transformational learning can help you focus attention on how to ensure that your course's learning will be personal and lasting for students.

> By the end of this course, students will gain the following skills and understandings:
>
> - Understand and remember key concepts, terms, relationships, and so on;
> - Know how to use the content;
> - Be able to relate this subject to other subjects;
> - Understand the personal and social implications of knowing about this subject.
> - Care about the subject (and about learning more on the subject);
> - Know how to keep on learning about this subject after the course is over (p. 39).

Making Connections

Backward design and learner-centered teaching is about more than just developing sound learning outcomes—it's also important that your outcomes and the assignments are all *aligned* or connected. *Alignment* means that you aren't asking students to do anything that isn't connected to your larger goals. Your course materials, resources, and activities should all help students meet the course learning outcomes. For example, how does memorizing all the names of the characters in one of Shakespeare's plays help students gain conceptual understanding of renaissance drama? The alignment between the course outcomes and the assignments shouldn't just make sense to you; it should also make sense to your students. This involves more than simply going over your syllabus on the first day of the term, it means creating clear assignments and instructions that always point back to the learning goals for the course. Help students understand the purpose of each assignment and activity, how each assessment relates to the larger course goals, and what successful learning looks like for each activity.

Having clear alignment is necessary in all courses, but you will need to be even more explicit about your alignment in online or hybrid courses. Access is one of the consistent benefits of online or hybrid courses, but increased flexibility also means that these courses have an even greater need for the kind of careful design and structure that benefits student learning (Blaich et al., 2016; Haak et al., 2011; Supiano, 2018). In F2F classes, there are plenty of opportunities to respond to off-the-cuff questions from your students like, Why are we doing this? Or, What do I do next? However, hybrid and online instructors are not always present with their students at the same time, so they need to "ensure that their backward design floats a little closer to the surface, visible in multiple ways throughout the semester" (Darby & Lang, 2019, p. 10). The advantage of doing this work for online courses is that it will bring you even greater clarity when designing for F2F. Experienced instructors agree that the added attention to backward design and alignment in online teaching actually helps you to be a better instructor across modalities (Gannon, 2019).

One way to easily surface this alignment in your courses is to build a course map. If you've taught in a K-12 environment, these maps will be familiar to you from the curriculum mapping process. If not, a course map might remind you of a beefed-up course schedule with additional bells and whistles. Table 2 is a simple table-based course map that you can use as a template.

1. Start by listing your course's learning outcomes at the top.
2. Next, fill in all your assignments (or, evidence of student learning) in the Activities and Assignments column. In Chapter 6, you'll learn more about formative and summative assessments. For now, write down all the things students will do to show you their learning.
3. Last, think carefully about each activity and assignment and determine all of the steps a student will need to take in order to be successful. (You might even consider storyboarding all the steps a student would take.) Also, identify what campus resources the student might take advantage of to increase their likelihood of success (e.g., should they visit the campus writing center before turning in that paper? Should they work with peers to study for that test? Should they visit your office hours to get feedback on wrong answers from a problem set?). Add this information to the Learning Materials

column aligned with each respective assignment. This section is a great way for you to start being explicit with your students about how each activity in your course will support them in their learning. Help make this column more transparent for your students by clearly identifying which materials are required and which are supplemental.

Table 2 Simple Course Map

Course Learning Outcomes	Activities & Assignments	Learning Materials (Including Support or Resources for Further Learning)

If you are planning to teach an online or hybrid course, you will want to take a few more steps with your course map (see Table 3). Because these kinds of courses benefit from additional structure, it's helpful to break your course into modules, or weekly units, that enable your students to plan their time similar to how they plan their time in a F2F class. The module learning outcomes you create in this more detailed map make it clear to your students (each week) what you are doing and why. Below are directions to complete a course map with module and module learning outcomes:

1. Start by listing your course's learning outcomes at the top.
2. Next, fill in all your assignments (or, evidence of student learning) in the Activities and Assignments column.

3. Once you have determined what is acceptable evidence of student learning, start to chunk those activities and assignments into different units or modules to make the course more manageable. Name these in the Module/Unit column.
4. Closely examine your assignments and activities in each module or unit, and start to identify supporting learning outcomes and add them to the Module/Unit Learning Outcomes column. Use the same format you would use to write a course learning objective, create module or unit-level learning objectives that demonstrate how the assignments or activities a student completes within each module or unit will help them to build skills and knowledge to make progress toward the overarching course learning outcomes.
5. Think carefully about each activity and assignment and determine all of the steps a student will need to take in order to be successful. (You might even consider storyboarding all the steps a student would take.) Also, identify what campus resources the student might take advantage of to increase their likelihood of success (e.g., Should they visit the campus writing center before turning in that paper? Should they work with peers to study for that test? Should they visit your office hours to get feedback on wrong answers from a problem set?). Add this information to the Learning Materials column aligned with each respective assignment. This section is a great way for you to start being explicit with your students about how each activity in the course will support them in their learning. Help make this column more transparent for your students by clearly identifying which materials are required and which are supplemental.
6. Lastly, as a self-check, go through each module or unit and identify which course learning outcomes are supported by the materials, activities, and assessments in that module.

Add the number of the course-level student learning outcomes to the Aligned Learning Outcomes column. Double check yourself to make sure there isn't excess material or activities that don't support your student learning outcomes.

Table 3 Online Course Map

Course Learning Outcomes
1.
2.
3.

Activities & Assignments	Module/Unit	Module/Unit Learning Outcomes	Learning Materials (Including Support or Resources for Further Learning)	Aligned Learning Outcome

When you are doing this for the first time, we encourage you to use a format that clearly shows the alignment between your student learning goals and the assignments. Once this table is complete, you should be able to see the arc of your course, all of the assignments you will use to measure student learning, and all of the materials students will need to be successful in the course. In later iterations, you can start to experiment with making the format more creative or engaging for your students. Perhaps you'd rather present this as an infographic, concept map, or interactive HTML page where students can click on assessments to see what kinds of materials or support they'll need to access. Over the course of several semesters you might even solicit feedback from your classes and add student voices to this document to highlight strategies that previous students found helpful or materials they found most useful.

Once you have your course map in place, there is one more step to completing your design process: designing a communication plan based on your course map. This plan should help you identify key touchpoints when all your students could use a little extra attention. This extra help might look like a time period for conferences, a weekly summary or bridge video, key moments when you want students to reflect on their work and plan for their final projects or exams. This communication plan isn't something that you need to share with your students, but it's helpful for you to have in place so you aren't blindsided during a busy term with student questions or concerns. Try to identify early stages where you'd want to catch struggling students to ensure they too can access a pathway to success in your course. These communications can have the greatest impact when they occur before midterm. If you are teaching online or hybrid courses, ask yourself how you will communicate your presence in the course and guide students through all the exciting work you have planned. What might an orientation to your online course look like? How should a student plan to navigate your course materials and what strategies can they use to engage with them more deeply? What sorts of regular feedback loops can a student expect from you and how can the student connect with other members of the class? This communication plan will help you crystalize your expectations for success in your course and translate that clearly to your students.

Special Considerations in Online Course Design

Teaching online can make tangible, and often textual, many of the interactions in the class. In this more durable format, class discussions are captured in a discussion forum, directions are captured in written assignments and can be clarified by recorded screen capture videos, and classroom identities are constructed through avatars and feedback loops (Major, 2015). Depending on your institution, the course may even persist in a read-only format after the term has closed so that students can continue to return to the materials and conversations to refresh their understanding. A thoughtfully designed online course, where the smaller steps for learning such as homework, journals, or practice problems lead to larger and more complex artifacts of learning such as portfolios or exams, can preserve both the "artifacts" and the "processes" of learning (Major, 2015, p. 67). The opportunity that the online course affords does not mean that it's necessarily easy to make these very important features of your course visible. In fact, the process of explaining each step of an assignment, or clearly articulating links between concepts, is some of the most challenging work we do as educators. Teaching online means that we are also helping students to learn new material in an (often) unfamiliar learning environment, and as they acquire "skill[s] to become expert as a virtual student" (Ubell, 2017, p. 5). Although most students will graduate having completed at least one online class, they have generally had all (or, at least the majority) of their previous learning experiences in physical classrooms (Miller, 2014). Even students who took classes during the COVID-19 health crisis may not have experienced a thoughtfully designed online course depending on the resources their institution had and their instructors' preparation (Hodges et al., 2020). Instead, students are more familiar with classes that have clear start and end times and physical materials and that are held in a room with other people. As a result, in our online classes "it may not be clear where to start, how to spend one's study time, or when the work is due" (Miller, 2014, p. 28). The online course also tends to have a larger quantity of written material than its F2F counterparts. Students who struggle with deep reading skills may fall behind in the online course or overly rely on F2F interactions in a hybrid course (Miller, 2014).

Whether you teach F2F, online, or hybrid courses, all classes benefit from this deep understanding of your learning outcomes and attention to design. If you weren't sure whether your course structure matters, believe us (and the consensus of higher education research), it probably matters more than you know. The following chapters will help you see your course as a cohesive project with clear goals, steps for students to achieve those goals, strategies for helping students become lifelong learners, and reflective strategies that will help you to improve your teaching.

KEY TAKEAWAYS

- If you have the freedom to design your own course, always start with what you want students to learn by the end—jot down the things they need to know or be able to do—and start your planning with these goals in mind.
- Rewrite or rearrange prescribed learning outcomes in your own words. They will only be useful to you and your students if you understand them.
- Use a course map or outline to check your design against your course's learning goals and outcomes to make sure there is a clear purpose to everything you're asking students to do.

CHAPTER 3

HOW CAN YOU CREATE A WELCOMING CLASSROOM COMMUNITY?

Imagine the following: it's the first day of the semester and a student walks into a large, impersonal classroom where other students sit silently. The student is taking this course because it's required, and they are not confident in their abilities. The instructor is at the front of the class, busy with his notes. Once class begins, he hands out the syllabus and proceeds to read aloud a series of cautions (don't fall behind, don't cheat, don't hand in late work). A couple of students who already know each other exchange glances. The professor seems to know one student and makes a couple of joking remarks to her. He makes no effort to learn other students' names. As the weeks pass the student struggles but doesn't feel comfortable asking other students for help or contacting the instructor. A couple of times during class the instructor asks if anyone has any questions and although the student does have questions, they don't want to be embarrassed in front of the other students who all seem to understand the material. Instead, the student tries their best to learn the material on their own and struggles. They dread the class but work as hard as they can on their own, manage to pass the course with a C-, and never think about the course or the material again.

The scenario described above might seem like an exaggeration, but it is how many college students experience their courses, and it certainly is not confined to any one discipline. It's not even the worst-case scenario, which would be when a student fails the course and ends up dropping out of college. In our last chapter we discussed what to consider when designing your course. In the next few chapters, we will focus on what happens once the class begins, when you leave the realm of the hypothetical and meet the actual people who will be your students. This is where teaching becomes unpredictable, sometimes nerve-wracking, but also inspiring. Teaching, whether online or F2F, is a craft that is learned over time; however, research on learning as a social act and the importance of belonging and teacher immediacy can help us understand how we might approach this complex task of helping a group of strangers form a learning community. We'll help you understand why creating a welcoming environment is one of the most valuable things you can accomplish at the outset of your course, and we'll invite you to take the steps necessary to build a framework that makes this kind of learning community possible.

Let's return to the hypothetical student above. The instructor described in the scenario above might be very concerned with their students' success. However, they haven't created a welcoming environment where students feel comfortable asking for help or learning from each other. What could they have done to increase the struggling student's chance of greater success? To start, they could have welcomed students to the class by making eye contact and trying to learn their names from the first day. They could have worked to create more welcoming language in their syllabus so that it did not read like a list of don'ts and they might have helped students to engage in the course content by explaining how the course content might affect their own lives and majors. They might have sacrificed 20 minutes during one of the first classes to engage students in an icebreaker activity, so that students felt more comfortable with each other. They might have built into the course time for group work where students collaborate on problems or answered discussion questions, allowing students to realize that everyone struggles and potentially leading to out-of-class study groups. Instead of merely asking if there are "any questions" (one of the least effective techniques to solicit questions) they could have polled students or asked for a 2-minute response paper as a way of ascertaining whether students understood a concept before moving on. Instead of holding "office hours" they could hold "help hours" at the campus coffee shop or a less intimidating environment.

Some of you may be wondering, what does this social/emotional work have to do with teaching the course material? Despite our culture's emphasis on individual achievement, many educational theorists argue that learning is inherently a social process.[1] Learning does not depend solely on the textbook or the assignments; it also depends on the people around us and how comfortable we feel in the environment. Joshua Eyler summarizes it nicely: "Our bonds with other people are an integral part of being human, and they are the starting point for the way we experience the world" (2018, p. 67). We learn from our peers, from engaging with others, and our learning is affected by these social relationships. Perhaps the most salient work on social learning comes from Lev Vygotsky and his concept of the zone of proximal development, which he describes as "the distance between the actual developmental level as determined by individual problem solving and the level of potential development as determined through problem solving under adult guidance or in collaboration with capable peers" (1980). The idea is that learners have a broader range of potential when they learn with others than if they only ever attempt to learn on their own. In short, by learning together we expand one another's potential. More recent research in student success indicates that students have the best chance of realizing the added potential of learning in a community when they *feel connected* to someone or a group. In other words, students' learning and long-term success in college depends on their feelings of belonging in the classroom (Walton & Cohen, 2011). A long-term study of students at a private liberal arts college showed that personal relationships had the most significant impact on college students' success (Chambliss & Takacs, 2014). For the growing number of older, commuting, or returning students who don't live on campus, the classroom community becomes the most important environment for friendships and connections to develop. Although learning is distinct from persistence, students who feel connected (and as a result more comfortable) in the classroom, are better able to perform than if they are learning on their own or feeling isolated in the environment. In short, our feelings impact the way that we learn. Students who aren't distracted by feeling isolated or unsure of their place in the classroom will have greater cognitive resources to apply to the learning at hand. Our aim then is to create a classroom that encourages students to feel a sense of belonging and connectedness so that they can best realize their potential not only in your course but in their college experience.

Cultivating Community by Being a Good Host

One way to start thinking about cultivating a welcoming community in your classroom is to start thinking about how you will model it. Small gestures convey a lot. When the Dalai Lama and Archbishop Desmond Tutu planned to meet in Dharamasala in 2015 for a series of talks between the two aging spiritual leaders on the topic of joy, the Dalai Lama met the Archbishop at the airport. On the first day of their historic dialogues, he paused the conversation after a deep dive into how one can still find joy in a world of injustice so that they could take tea. Later, when they sat down to lunch, the 88-year-old exiled leader passed the homemade bread and double checked that the temperature was comfortable for his guests (Dalai Lama, Tutu, & Abrams, 2016). In short, he was a good host. With a flurry of monks, devotees, and organizers, the Dalai Lama could have left any of these small attentions up to staff and concerned himself only with his daily prayers and the spiritual dialogues he and the Archbishop were having. He could have left the subtle but important work of hosting and showing concern for his guests' physical and emotional comfort to others and focused only on the intellectual exchange. You might see a parallel in professors who attest that they don't want to know anything personal about their students, or that they only want to hear from students about the course topic. The Dalai Lama, on the other hand, spent valuable time and energy in making sure his guests felt welcome. His message of humanity was illuminated by his ability to relate to his guests as fellow humans in the most basic ways.

You certainly don't need to be a venerated spiritual leader to know what it feels like to be welcomed and made comfortable by a good host. You may also know what it's like to show up and feel completely lost at a professional or social gathering. Conflict resolution expert and professional facilitator Priya Parker makes a thorough investigation of the benefits of a thoughtful host, and she warns against the host who shies away from their responsibilities because they are uncomfortable with the perception that they are in charge. It's not that she believes a good host must be an authoritarian, but instead a good host needs to recognize that the role comes with a responsibility to the group. Parker describes the first day of Harvard professor Ronald Heiftetz's class on adaptive leadership to clarify her point. Heifetz sits in a chair not making eye contact with students and not saying or doing anything. A few uncomfortable moments ensue: "Without the professor leading the way, the students must deal with one another. Any of the 100 of them is, technically, free to speak (or yell or dance or laugh or attempt to take charge" (Parker, 2018, p. 76). And yet, the painfully awkward conversation that takes place among the students doesn't reveal a balance of power, or what we are aiming for with a classroom community. Without the professor's guidance, other kinds of power relationships play out. Those who feel entitled to speak up do so, and those who feel entitled to tell others to be quiet also do so; some students feel entitled to proclaim their inconvenience, and some students clearly don't feel comfortable saying anything at all. When Heifetz eventually begins the class, his short experiment has enabled him to make his point: You can't "eradicate power" by resigning leadership (Parker, 2018, p. 76). Like water without a container, power will just find another well-worn course. Without your guidance and structure, students who are marginalized outside of class most likely will feel marginalized in your class.

It's completely normal to feel uneasy about your role in

the classroom and uncomfortable acknowledging the power and responsibility you have as an instructor. Your feelings also aren't isolated to being a graduate instructor. According to Parker's experience, it's common for hosts to try to abdicate their responsibilities in settings ranging from policy symposia to housewarming parties. "This is because to talk about their role is to talk about their power as a host," Parker explains, "and to talk about that power is to acknowledge that it exists" (2018, p. 72). Power doesn't have to mean dominance, though. Recall the Dalai Lama's small acts of generosity, and his sense of responsibility to his guests; think of how he made the human connection as important as the intellectual exchange.

Being a good host allows you to spend less time thinking about your insecurities, and more time focused on the needs of your students. When meeting a class for the first time in person, a lot of us feel nervous about mundane things, like what to wear, exactly when to arrive at the classroom, and how to introduce ourselves. It's normal, even useful, to feel a bit nervous on the first day of the semester. When we get too nervous, however, we often become overly focused on our own behavior rather than paying attention to our students. Have you ever seen a presentation where something goes awry (a technical glitch or some missing materials)? Savvy presenters keep things moving with what they have, but sometimes the presenter gets so anxious about the hiccup that they keep circling back to it for the rest of the presentation ("Well, you would see my point better if I had been able to show you the graphs," or "This would have been way better with the audio"). When this happens the group also doesn't have a chance to move past the hiccup, and everyone is left feeling the same discomfort felt by the presenter. Hiccups happen and you will definitely get nervous, but focusing your attention on your students will prevent you from crowding the room with your own feelings.[2]

One way to make sure that you can project calm—even when you don't feel it—is to have a plan. A welcoming instructor carefully prepares those first few minutes of class and has an outline of what they will do. This plan will keep you focused on your students and help them to know what to do to be successful in the course. We've given you a sample agenda below that can be adapted to suit your course. At its core, your first-day plan should help your students make a connection to the course topic, it should help you to connect with your students, and it should enable them to connect to one another. In an F2F course, your first day could look something like this:

1. Introduce the course topic and its current relevance. Has anything from the course shown up in the news lately? Are there any new discoveries in the field? How will the course help them to achieve their own academic or personal goals? Depending on the topic, you might even ask students to share what they already (think) they know about the topic. (10 minutes)
2. Introduce yourself and express your interest or passion for the topic. Why are you here? What are you excited about? What can students expect from you? (5 minutes)
3. Help students connect with each other with a small group activity. (25 minutes) (see the exercise in co-constructing course expectations below for an example.)
4. Take time to answer questions and clarify what students need to do before the next class. (10 minutes)

In an online or hybrid course, all these elements can be captured in a welcome module, an activity, and a place to learn more about each other. What you do on the first day of your course will set the tone, convey your teaching persona, and give students a sense of what they can expect from the course. You'll notice that we don't recommend that you waste this important opportunity by merely reading the syllabus aloud. Use your first contact with students as an opportunity to start building community and to motivate students by explaining the value of the course to their academic careers and to their lives outside of school. If having the students read the syllabus carefully during the first week of the semester is important to you, give them an online quiz or a short writing prompt about the syllabus. In the section on co-constructing expectations, we'll share an activity that also encourages students to dig into the syllabus while making connections with their peers. There are a number of ways to help students thoroughly understand the complexities of your course without reading the syllabus to them.

Instead of focusing on the syllabus, we recommend starting out by talking about the big picture: Why does your course matter and how will it help students achieve their own goals? Elaine Showalter describes using the first day of her literature course to give students highlights of all the novels they will be reading, like the previews that begin a film (2003). David Gooblar suggests pretending the first day is the last and giving students the conclusion to the course (2019, p. 61). Consider showing students a problem they'll be able to solve with the knowledge they gain in your course. In addition to expressing your enthusiasm for the subject and the course, this gives students an opportunity to make their own connections between their goals and the course. After all, they are the experts on themselves and their goals. This is also a way to get to know your students. Research shows that when students themselves connect the course to their own future goals, their motivation increases. This type of goal setting can also reduce achievement gaps for minoritized students (Schippers et al., 2015). One variation on the schedule above would be to spend 3–5 minutes in the first part of class having students write down how their success in this course will directly affect a future goal and listing any obstacles they anticipate to their success. You can collect these to review and bring them back to the students at key moments throughout the course—they can be motivating in the weeks leading up to a large project or test. Or, they can be used at the end of the course to help students reflect on the progress they have made.

After you've taken a look at the big picture, introduce yourself by telling students a bit about your background. Put yourself in their shoes: What would *you* want to know about your instructor that would make you feel confident about the semester ahead? Don't be afraid of being sincere or corny—this is not the time to be ironic, cynical, or aloof. Tell them why you've decided to devote a considerable portion of your life to your discipline; let them know that you've thought carefully about the design of the course and that you're excited to get to know them. If it seems appropriate, you can share with them any unique experiences you have with the subject. Have you attended any field schools, labs, or professional events that inform this subject? If you're funny, crack a joke. If you're comfortable mentioning your own personal life, say something about your interests outside of class. Again, if you're comfortable, share a difficulty you encountered when you were an undergraduate and tell them how you surmounted it. Some instructors invite students to ask them questions. The specific information isn't as important as the gesture of being open and approachable. Look at each student when they talk, and carefully consider their questions. Don't cut them off in mid-sentence—you'd be surprised at how often instructors do this out of nervousness. If you're teaching online, you can tackle many of these topics in your welcome video. Keep it short, but don't be afraid to present yourself as a whole person, not just a content expert. The video doesn't need to be fancy or super professional, just welcoming (Darby & Lang, 2019, p. 91). If this is your first time teaching, you might not want to share this information; instead, tell them how long you've been studying the subject and why you believe that your discipline provides an important way to look at the world. Students respond to an instructor's enthusiasm. Aeron remembers being a freshman at Binghamton University where the graduate teaching assistant for a world politics class told them that he decided to forego law school in order to study with the professor. His commitment to the subject and his excitement to be working with the professor was palpable. It also humanized the teaching assistant; instead of being her instructor he became someone making hard choices about his own life and career.

The next part—helping your students connect to one another—is often a lot of fun and a great way for you to learn more about them and what's brought them to your class. Depending on who your students are, you'll want to adjust your approach. If you are working primarily with first-year students, or it's an introductory course, use some icebreakers to help students get comfortable just interacting in class. Stephanie would often have students arrange themselves in a line by who had to travel the shortest or longest distance to get to class that day. It often started with a lot of noise and chaos, but in a few minutes students had found the right order, interacted with at least two people, and learned a little something about their peers. Students would then introduce themselves to those on their left and right, and they already had something in common to talk about—who doesn't have a complaint or two about their commute? The question doesn't matter as much as the idea that students can line themselves up on a low-stakes topic: it could be where their birthdays fall in the year, how many languages they speak, or how many pets they have (Gonzalez, 2015). For a large class, you might treat this icebreaker as an informal debate. Ask students a series of either/or questions and have them arrange themselves on the side of the room they agree with (e.g., Do you prefer cats or dogs? Do you think horoscopes are hokey or cool? Would you rather go to the beach or the mountains? Do you brush your teeth first thing or after breakfast?). Another variation on this icebreaker has students gather in groups or in corners of the room based on their answer to multiple-choice questions. For example, which is your favorite: (a) horror movies, (b) romcoms, (c) action movies, or (d) animated films?

Upperclassmen or students in a course for majors may be tired of icebreakers. Instead, engage these students in activities that are directly related to the course material. You can build on the conversation you have with students about the big picture to help them better understand how their knowledge and experience might inform the class. Some instructors ask students to complete "concept inventories" in small groups in order to gauge their preconceptions and understanding of course material. It also gets them thinking about the material before they officially encounter it (the science of learning calls this *predicting*). An article in the *Chronicle of Higher Education* has an excellent description of how various instructors help students make these connections collaboratively on day one: an historian gives students packets of primary source material to examine and discuss; a writing instructor has students reflect on a piece of writing that impacted them; an upper-level psychology course has students work in small groups to complete an assignment that tests their understanding of the human brain (Lang, 2019). All these activities could happen in pairs or small groups depending on your class size. If the course is small enough, students might simply share with the entire group. The point here is to help students see themselves as part of a community of learners where they will be learning from you and from one another. Interacting with each other in class increases the chances of students helping each other and decreases the chance that a student will view their struggles in the course as unique or, even worse, as a reason they cannot succeed.

The strategies above will get you through your agenda, but you'll also want to take a few steps to make sure you are comfortable with your plan. If you're teaching face-to-face, we suggest finding the classroom the week before and getting a sense of the space. Does the technology work? Are the desks or chairs arranged in the best way? Can they even be moved? Does the classroom have chalk or markers, or should you plan to bring your own? It won't take you long to discover the answers to these questions, and you'll feel more comfortable and confident as a result.

Immediacy

This planning will certainly help you to focus on your students. The next skill—teacher immediacy—is a skill you can practice that will help you sustain a welcoming classroom community throughout the semester. A teacher's *immediacy* is her presence and attentiveness in the classroom. You can think of immediacy as a kind of invitation to interact. When you meet with someone for the first time, their immediacy is what makes you feel comfortable continuing to interact with them, and it's likely what made you approach them in the first place. According to research, immediacy helps you form a strong rapport with your students and can increase their motivation to learn, their attendance, even the time they spend studying (Richmond et al., 2016; Handelsman et al., 2005).

How do you develop teacher immediacy? Some of you might already have strong interpersonal skills, but if not, it is possible to improve them. When teaching in the classroom, learn your students' preferred names/pronouns and their pronunciation, smile, use gestures when you speak, try to use the tone of your voice to illustrate your excitement or your interest, make eye contact, and move around the classroom; all these actions help students feel that you are present and attentive. It is totally OK to fake it until you make it with this strategy. It might feel excruciating to you to make small-talk with students before or after class. That's fine. Have a question or two handy to help you out when your mind goes blank (What do they think is the best food on campus? Or, where is the best cheap parking?). The main point is to show your students that you are paying attention to them and open to them approaching you for help. It's not far off from the ways people make themselves approachable in any group setting. Stephanie has worked a lot of service and support jobs throughout her career, and the secret she always shares with people is that if someone trusts you enough to ask you a menial question then they are more likely to trust you with a larger one. If students find you approachable and helpful for small questions like directions to the library, then you are more likely to build the rapport necessary for them to trust your feedback on their classwork or for them to come to you when they are struggling.

While immediacy can feel more challenging in an online class, the strategies for creating it can be far more concrete. Immediacy is often referred to as *instructor presence* in an online course, and you can cultivate it by using regular, timely communications to help students feel like you are supporting their journey every time they log into the course. There are many variations on this theme, but generally speaking you'll want to provide students with a clear and personal welcome message, and, each week, provide them with some communication that looks ahead to the week they are starting and connects back to the work they just completed. For the beginning of your course, you can record a welcome video. To keep up this instructor presence, you can use weekly communications with text, images, or audio to catch students' attention and help generate some interest in the week's topics and work. These communications can also help students make sense of the work they've completed so far. In an F2F discussion you would likely tie student comments together to help them build on one another's ideas. In an online class, you can use your weekly communications to quote or paraphrase from students' discussion boards or assignments to point out new discoveries in the course or thoughtful observations about the content. If students are working in smaller discussion groups, see if there are themes running across the groups or major distinctions among their approaches. Your attention to their work will help them to know that someone is listening when they put their work out there in the course. This strategy is particularly helpful if you can also point to how students can question or continue to build on these discoveries in the next assignment or module.

This often helps students see the progress they are making and understand how the stages of their work fit together.

One of the simplest ways you can demonstrate immediacy in any course is by learning your students' names and using them regularly. If your college includes students' photos with the roster, you can start learning their names before the first day of class. If you aren't sure how to pronounce someone's name, let them know that it's important to you to get it right and ask them to pronounce it for you. Consider using free apps like HowtoPronounce.com or NameCoach, which allow students to pronounce their names and add them to a digital class profile. You might even try to normalize helping the class with pronunciation by coming up with a helpful device (Stephanie often tells people her last name rhymes with ping pong to help them say it correctly). Even if you are a teaching assistant for a very large lecture section, you can still learn students' names. On the first day, have each student write their name (in bold, clear letters) on a piece of paper and take a picture of the whole class. (It's important to let students know you will be taking their photo and how you plan to use it, and to allow anyone to opt out if they'd prefer not to be photographed.) Try to learn three–five names before each class. You don't have to memorize all of them but addressing a few students by their names each class can help contribute to a stronger sense of community despite the large class size. Aeron had a colleague who taught an enormous introduction to psychology course who used this technique and by the end of the semester usually learned about 75% of his students' names; students remark on this years later.

Inviting Students to Co-Construct the Experience

Another effective way to create community and strengthen student engagement is to invite students to be co-constructors of the course. You can start this process by having students come to consensus around a set of expectations for your engagements and theirs. Aeron does this with every undergraduate and graduate course she teaches. First, explain to the students that you'd like their input in order to establish a productive classroom learning community. Next, ask students to form groups of four to five: this can be done F2F or online, in large lecture courses as well as small seminars. Ask them to generate a list of five expectations for classroom behavior, or, alternatively, suggestions for how you can best help them learn in the class. Aeron often primes the pump by mentioning that past classes have asked that she return papers/tests within a certain time period, or that students arrive on time and wait to enter the room if another student is presenting, etc. Once student groups have generated their five suggestions, ask for a volunteer from each group to present the group's suggestions while you record them. You can respond in real time to some of their suggestions. For example, if students request that their papers be returned within a week, you might let them know that because of your teaching load you won't be able to get papers back within one week, but pledge to get them back in two. Or you could collect all the groups' suggestions, thank them, and then use a few minutes of the next class to summarize their ideas and then respond. This activity can be done in online classes with break-out groups (for synchronous classes) or with software such as Padlet.

This activity can help you to learn about their expectations and strengthen their sense of agency in their own learning. Motivation increases with choice and relevancy: a student (or anybody, really) performs better when they have some control over their work and that work has a connection to their own lives (Pekrun, 2006). You will learn a lot about your students' past educational experiences by doing this activity. When students request that they not be "humiliated" when they contribute to class discussions and that assignments be returned before the subsequent assignment is due, they reveal past negative classroom experiences. This collaborative activity could be replicated to help the class decide how to tackle a particular project, or you could even use it to allow students to suggest supplemental reading materials for the course. By allowing students to directly contribute to decision making in the course, you can show students that their hard work will pay off, give them some choices in how they can work, and provide opportunities for students to connect the material to their own lives. Research suggests that students from lower socioeconomic backgrounds often develop a skepticism about whether their efforts will result in positive outcomes (Wilkinson & Pickett, 2009), so providing these opportunities for agency can be particularly valuable in helping the entire class understand what kinds of efforts will yield success. These kinds of activities enable students to engage with each other in an authentic way as knowledgeable participants who have things to contribute to the shared learning of the course on day one. In doing this, you signal to students that you are open to their input, and you also ask students to share in the responsibility for the success of the course.

Challenges to Belonging

There are some things you'll want to be aware of as you're planning to create a welcoming environment. If you've never questioned that you belong in higher education or if you see learning as an individual undertaking, you might wonder why classroom community matters so much. Your own experience as a college student may shape how familiar you are with threats to classroom community, such as microaggressions or uneven access to basic resources. For example, did you know that a significant number of college students experience food insecurity and homelessness? Sara Goldrick-Rab, Founder of the Hope Center at Temple University, estimates that 36% of university students and 56% of community college students go without meals, often having to decide between buying course supplies and buying food (Goldrick-Rab et al., 2018). Whether you are teaching at a wealthy private university or at a community college, food scarcity, homelessness, and lack of family support can manifest in the classroom as lack of attention or low motivation. Your students' physical, mental, and emotional health profoundly affects how they show up in your class. We're not recommending that you become a social worker for your students, but you can remember to think of your students as whole human beings. Their learning depends on their physical, mental, and emotional health. And it's a safe bet to assume that you don't fully understand the circumstances, challenges, or motivations of students you've just met. As one graduate teaching assistant noted, "I was shocked when I learned my students' course loads, the number of hours they worked, and their family responsibilities!"

Harvard Education Professor Anthony Jack has written about his own experience as a low-income minoritized student attending an affluent private college far from his community. He describes how the economic disparities between him and other students produced feelings of profound alienation (Jack, 2019). Jack remembers the food desert his campus became during university breaks when wealthier students left and the cafeterias shuttered, while he stayed to pick up extra shifts at his campus job. He recalls the cognitive dissonance he felt studying safely in his dorm room while receiving phone calls from his extended family who were processing neighborhood tragedy and violence: "I always wondered, unnerved, just how close my family was to whatever prompted such a call. I was away. They were still there." As much as you believe your course to be an opportunity for students to learn, we never quite know what students are giving up to attend our classes, who they are supporting, and who counts on them for child-care, financial support, or transportation.

The Benefits of Creating Community

The time and effort it takes to establish a classroom community is more than offset when we consider how much energy it takes to salvage a bad classroom dynamic. The first step is to realize that you are teaching specific students, not some idealized vision of how students ought to be. Your students bring a variety of personalities, abilities, preconceptions and strengths to the class. We encourage you to start from a place of curiosity about your students. Who are these individuals listed on your roster? What can you tell about them: their names, majors, what high schools they attended, where did they grow up? What other languages do they know? How might their own experiences and cultures contribute to the course? You can start finding the answers to these questions by beginning your class with some of the activities in this chapter, and you'll want to continue building opportunities for them to share as the semester continues.

As high as the stakes may be for you as a new instructor, in most cases the stakes are even higher for your students. Your effect as a teacher is profound and extensive; your class has the power to spark interest in your field, to teach them important skills and habits, and to inspire confidence in themselves. Conversely, your class could make a student feel that they don't belong in college, that they shouldn't pursue a particular major, or that the material doesn't matter to their lives. As you continue teaching, we suspect that you will someday encounter a former student you barely remember who will tell you that your course changed their life in some way. The students you will teach as a graduate student most likely will be freshmen and sophomores, those who are most at risk for dropping out (and ending up saddled with student loans but no degree). You don't have to be a tenured professor to start thinking about your responsibility to your students, to create an environment where students feel connected to the material, their peers, and to you as the instructor.

KEY TAKEAWAYS

- Plan to help students connect with you, one another, and the course content in the first week of the semester.
- Remember that small gestures, like knowing student names and asking for their input in class decisions, can have a big impact.
- Don't take it personally if a student disengages, as we don't always know why. Know your campus resources so that you can refer a student should they need help.

CHAPTER 4

HOW DO YOU DEVELOP A CLASSROOM PRACTICE?

Medical experiments can be stopped because an intervention has such an outsized benefit to patients that it would be unethical to continue withholding the beneficial treatment from the control group. But what about teaching methods? The authors of one of the most comprehensive meta-analyses of active learning in STEM show the overwhelming benefits of active learning techniques on student learning. They even argue that "If the experiments analyzed here had been conducted as randomized controlled trials of medical interventions, they may have been stopped for benefit—meaning that enrolling patients in the control condition might be discontinued because the treatment being tested was clearly more beneficial" (Freeman et al., 2014, p. 8413).[1] All the tips and advice we provide you in the rest of the chapter are inflected by the thorough consensus across the education landscape that students learn the most when they actively participate in constructing knowledge—and don't just sit and listen. After you've spent some time getting to know your students in the first week, those same strategies from the previous chapter can be excellent guideposts throughout the semester: for each week or unit, consider how you will connect with your students, connect them to the material, and help them make connections with one another. In this chapter we'll explain how to develop active learning strategies that are appropriate for your discipline, use mini lectures, prepare students for better discussions, and apply student feedback to your teaching.

So what exactly is active learning and why aren't these techniques the standard way of teaching? Contrary to how it might sound, active learning isn't about your students' physical activity nor does it refer to one specific teaching technique; according to Bonwell and Eison's definition (1991, p. iii) active learning "engages students in the process of learning through activities and/or discussion in class, as opposed to passively listening to an expert. It emphasizes higher-order thinking and often involves group work." Active learning allows students to try out their knowledge and understanding in frequent and low-stakes ways; it gives students lots of chances to practice being a member of your discipline and develop the know-how to be successful. We often employ nonactive learning techniques because this was the way we were taught. So, how do you know if you are engaging your students in active learning? The following two questions can help:

1. Are students asked to generate knowledge or ideas independently, and will they get feedback on those ideas in some way?
2. Are students given the opportunity to learn from or teach one another?

If you can answer "yes" to either question, then you are likely designing an active learning activity. For bonus points, you can also ask yourself whether students have a chance to reflect on their learning in the activity. *Metacognition*, or thinking about our thinking, helps students to identify how their actions are impacting their learning (positively or negatively) and improves the possibility of skill and knowledge transfer in more advanced learning (Chick, n.d.).

Creating a Class Plan

One way to avoid nonactive learning techniques is to create a class plan. Don't worry about scripting every word, which would likely lead to you focusing on the paper in front of you and not on your students and their reactions. Instead, prepare an outline for each class or weekly module—if you used the course map from Chapter 2 then you are likely off to a good start with your outline. If not, this outline does not have to be a formal lesson plan, but it should include the main points you want to cover or questions you want to ask. The other reason we don't encourage you to write out a script for your class is that it might encourage you to rely too much on lecturing at your students, which isn't the most effective way for students to learn. Does this mean that lectures are always a bad form of teaching? Not necessarily. Some of you are in disciplines where lecturing is a valued and established method of teaching; however, there is strong evidence that involving students in their learning results in deeper learning (Freeman et al., 2014). A recent study at Harvard showed that students learned more from active learning than from listening to a lecture, even though many of them thought they learned more from the lecture (Deslauriers et al., 2019).

While research confirms that active learning increases student understanding, we also recognize that your department may use other measures to define good teaching. Many of us would like to emulate the powerful lecturers who engaged and inspired us as college students. And, because many college professors were taught to see teaching excellence through the lens of an engaging lecture and have invested time in honing their own lecturing skills, the struggle between lecturing and active learning can become quite polarized and can put new instructors—particularly graduate students—in a difficult situation. While good teaching is rooted in the growth of your students, we recognize that your teaching opportunities and possibly even job prospects may rely on your capacity to engage students *and* to deliver a well-constructed lecture.

One strategy that will allow you to fulfill departmental expectations while still building a learner-centered teaching practice is the *mini lecture*. The skillful use of mini lectures combined with activities where students apply or engage with the material is an excellent way to begin your teaching practice. For example, let's say your class topic is the Industrial Revolution in England. You will likely assign students to read a textbook chapter or primary source before they come to class that day. If you then spend the class lecturing on material they have already read, you de-incentivize students to come prepared. Instead, you might begin class by asking students to write for five minutes on a prompt, such as, "Why did the Industrial Revolution occur in England first?" This kind of low-stakes writing exercise gets students to recall the information from their reading. Next, ask students to share their responses in pairs and then ask a couple of the pairs to summarize their discussion to the whole class. By writing their individual thoughts first, each student has a chance to reflect on the course material on their own, which means that students are held accountable for coming to class having completed the assigned reading. It also allows students to articulate their thoughts on the topic first and stimulates their interest so that they are more engaged in your mini lecture. In addition, this method gives quieter, more reflective students a chance to compose their thoughts before being asked to jump into a large discussion. After you hear from several students, and answer questions and correct misconceptions, then you can move on to a fifteen-minute mini lecture on the conditions of England that produced the Industrial Revolution. In the last five minutes, ask students to list questions that remain. Ending class by asking students to articulate remaining questions or muddiest points will give you a good way to measure what landed with the students and what is still unclear. Use your last five minutes to get students thinking about the work they need to complete for the next class; this is a great time to remind them about any projects they should be working on and what support resources might be available to them, and to make a purposeful connection between what they did that day and what they will do in the next class. An outline for this class might look like this:

1. Prewriting: Why did the Industrial Revolution occur in England first? (5 minutes)
2. Small groups: Synthesize findings, elect a group representative to share out. (10 minutes)
3. Share-out with class: (10 minutes)
4. Mini lecture: (15 minutes)
    a. Technological advances in England: steam engine and railroad
    b. New urban working class

5. Low-stakes writing: (5 minutes)
    a. What questions remain about the transition from rural economy to urban factories in the early 1800s?
6. Next class: (5 minutes)
    a. Reminders: rough drafts for essays are due next week, office hours and the writing center are great places to go for feedback, when reading Charles Dickens' *Hard Times*, consider his depiction of Coketown as a representation of the new urban, industrial town. Be prepared to discuss his representation with a passage from the novel.

You might be teaching a class where students' need to solve problems or respond to case studies. In those scenarios, you could alter the outline above:

1. Preassessment: show students a problem or case and have them work out a solution based on their reading or homework. (5 minutes)
2. Small groups: come to consensus on the steps to the problem or the case study response. (5 minutes)
3. Large group: Hear from the groups and discuss the solution or appropriate case study response. (5 minutes)
4. Instructor mini lecture: Clear up misconceptions and walk students through real-world applications. (5 minutes)
5. Small groups: give students a stretch problem that allows them to apply the skill to a slightly more challenging scenario. (5 minutes)
6. Large group: have each group walk the class through a step in the problem, or a stage in the process. (15 minutes)
7. Low-stakes writing: What questions remain? (5 minutes)
8. Next class: (5 minutes)

Because students are expected to generate knowledge independently at the start of each class, they are more likely to come to class having done the homework. (If you are concerned that this isn't the case, you can start collecting the work generated in that initial low-stakes writing and give it a check for completion.) Note that both these sample outlines have you shifting among student-generated knowledge, peer-generated knowledge, and instructor-generated knowledge. Familiarizing your students with a learning environment where new knowledge is coming from all three of these sources will help them to take greater agency in their learning as they move into more challenging coursework.

For those of you teaching large classes or multiple sections, the low-stakes writing mentioned above works well across these settings. In-class writings don't have to be corrected or graded, and you can quickly skim them and see where students' confusion lies. Low-stakes writing can be used as a strategy in just about any discipline, not just in writing-emphasis or Humanities courses. For example, an instructor of a math class might ask students to write a short reflection walking through the steps of solving a problem. In a chemistry course, the instructor might have students write out for themselves each step of an experiment. Students could compare these short reflections in small groups, and then surface incongruencies or questions to the larger class (Elder & Champine, 2016).

Planning in-person classes around the mini lecture will also prepare you well for online teaching. Your weekly plan in an online course can mirror the plan described above using low-stakes quizzes or surveys for getting the initial temperature check with student understanding; discussion boards to allow students to engage with one another, check their knowledge, and share ideas; and a short video or audio lecture from you to extend the conversation. You can wrap up the week with another short survey or journal reflection to give you a sense of the progress your students are making. There are many other strategies you can incorporate for an F2F or online course, but this foundation of the mini lecture paired with chances for engagement, individually and in groups, is a solid place to start.

Facilitating Discussions

If you are in a discipline where classroom discussion is valued and encouraged, how do you go about creating a good discussion? A truly engaged and on-point discussion, where every student presents their informed view on the topic and listens respectfully, and where ideas grow and develop, is a thing of beauty. It helps students explore diverse perspectives, increases "intellectual agility," helps them learn to communicate clearly, gets students invested in a topic, prepares them to engage in a democracy, and more (Brookfield & Preskill, 1999, p. 22–23). However, as Brookfield and Preskill acknowledge, "the chatter of student voices" alone does not mean that a productive or inclusive discussion is occurring (p. 20). A skilled discussion leader makes it look relatively effortless; however, it takes a lot of practice. The first step to having a productive class discussion is to explain the value of discussion to your students, many of whom may have experienced fruitless, unfocused discussions or discussions in which a couple of students dominated. Some students will feel cheated if the instructor isn't talking the whole time; after all, you are the expert—even if you don't feel like one yet! They may resent paying tuition to listen to the opinions of their fellow classmates. Tell students why you believe that discussion will help them learn and engage with the material. Explain that while you could happily talk for 50 minutes about the topic, talking to each other, defending their claims and listening to others' points of view, will help them learn that material in a richer way. Also, explain that you will structure the discussions so that they are productive and fair. If you're feeling ambitious, ask the students to help you create ground rules for discussion: ask them to describe (in writing) a time when they experienced a productive, enjoyable discussion and a time when they felt disappointed or disengaged with a discussion. Have students share their experiences in pairs or small groups and then create a document that lists the elements of a productive and unproductive discussion. Stephen Brookfield models a productive discussion by inviting a colleague to discuss a topic with him in front of the class (1999). If you're teaching online, you can post a model example of a good online discussion and explain why it's successful. Generally, a successful discussion includes students responding thoughtfully to each other, relating class material to their own lives or to current events, and building upon each other's ideas. Here are some guidelines for in-class discussion to share with students:

1. If you are someone who tends to talk a lot, practice waiting and allowing others to participate. (Stephanie is a talker in the classroom, so depending on the size of the group, she will try to wait for at least three other people to speak before she offers a contribution.)
2. Listen to understand. Do not interrupt or engage in side conversations when someone is talking.
3. If you're someone who tends to be quieter, challenge yourself to speak up more. Come to class with a question or comment prepared.

4. Realize that we all come to this class with different experiences, backgrounds, and beliefs. Don't use language or humor that puts other people down.
5. Disagree with a position, but do not make personal attacks.
6. Address your comments to other students, not just the instructor. Try to learn other students' names and refer to the points they made.
7. Realize that there are different strategies for solving problems and that other students may have something to teach you.

This is one example of a discussion guide, but you and your students might come up with more specifics depending on your campus culture or the current events of that semester.

Once you explain the benefits and establish ground rules, you will need to ensure that students are prepared for the discussion. Walking into a classroom and asking your students, "What did you think of last night's reading?" will rarely elicit a good discussion. In fact, without preparation, you might not elicit any response at all beyond comments from a couple of empathetic students who sense your desperation. A free-for-all discussion also tends to privilege the extroverted, glib, and those with educational and social capital. One way to help students prepare for class discussion is by giving them guided reading questions. First- and second-year students may not enter college with critical reading skills, and very few students will know how to be a reader in your discipline. We can lament this, but we should also offer some strategies for how they can read productively for your course. Guided reading questions also help students understand what information is most valuable to experts in your field, how they position arguments, and how they build knowledge. You could start the term by providing reading questions for students, directing them to focus on parts of the assigned material. You can simply use the same questions you plan to use for your discussion topics (this will also help you plan ahead). You can also incorporate students as peer facilitators of a discussion as they start to get a better handle on their reading and discussion skills. Ask facilitators to provide you with their discussion questions a week ahead of time so you can give them feedback and help them refine their questions. A general set of reading questions for an academic article or essay might include the following:

1. What central argument is made by the authors? And, what key points do they make to support that argument?
2. What key terms do you need to understand to make sense of this argument? Define them in your own words.
3. What evidence do the authors use? (Is it quantitative data, anecdotes, or metaphors?)
4. What points do you agree with and what points do you disagree with? Why? Use your own evidence to support your perspective.

For particularly dense writing, you might also have students start with a summary of each paragraph or create a graphic representation of the ideas and arguments (Bean, 2011, p. 179—180).

One of the most difficult parts of class discussion is holding your own fear of silence in check. Try not to interrupt a student or rush to explain without first asking the class for their thoughts. If the class is arranged in a circle, encourage them to address each other, not just you. You can do this by meeting a student's gaze and then directing it to the other students. Another technique is to paraphrase each student's comment—this works well if you have a larger class or if the chairs can't be put into a circle and thus students can't face each other and might not hear all comments. When you paraphrase, ask the student if you've correctly articulated what they meant. As you gain confidence, start noticing students' nonverbal cues. Are some students looking down at their phones? Has a student crossed their arms and pulled back from the group? Draw these students into the conversation by directing questions their way in a welcoming manner. At the end of a discussion, summarize it, pointing out the strengths or difficult issues discussed. Celebrate the hard work that the students achieved by pointing out how much was accomplished during the discussion. You may also assign each student a class discussion to summarize and post online: this is a wonderful way to archive the class discussion and to show students how much intellectual labor goes into a good discussion. It can also be helpful for students who missed class. Below are a few more ways you might start a discussion, adapted from Peter Frederick's essay on "The Dreaded Discussion: Ten Ways to Start" (1982):

- Goals and values testing: Ask students to determine the primary value of the day's reading for the course or topic in pairs or small groups. Frederick calls this a public "reality test" for your course goals. You can riff on this initial question by asking the groups to come up with relationships between the day's text and previous readings. You can provide students with prompts like the following:
  - Identify themes common to both texts.
  - Suggest the two most obvious differences between the two texts.
  - Which did you like best and why?
  - Make a list of as many comparisons (or contrasts) as you can in 10 minutes.

- Concrete images: Individually or in groups, have each student identify one concrete image/scene/event/moment from the text that stands out. They don't need to explain it or even say why it is important, they just need to identify it; you can list these on the board or a screen. Then, you can follow up with questions like the following:
  - What themes seem to emerge from these items?
  - What connects these images?
  - Is there a pattern to our recollected events?
  - What's missing?

  A variation on this is to have students go in order, each choosing a passage or event and linking it back to the person who went before them. Either approach allows every student to contribute in some way and prompts the class as a whole to concentrate on the reading at hand. This can be especially helpful with texts where there might be a lot of assumptions about the topic, but less familiarity with the actual text (like Mary Shelley's *Frankenstein* or discussions of stem cell research).
- Variations on having students generate their own discussion questions:
  - Have students write their questions on note cards and let one student choose the questions at random.
  - Have students write their questions on notecards or post on a shared screen and break into categories as a group.
  - Have students come to class with their question and serve as the discussion leader while the class addresses it.
  - Have each small group choose one big question to pose to the class. (Optional: they can facilitate the discussion while the class addresses it.)
- Generating truth statements: In small groups, have students generate three truth statements about the topic or reading. Example statements follow:

  - o It is true about reconstruction that . . . .
  - o We have agreed that it is true about the welfare system that . . . .
  - o It is true about international politics in the 1950s that. . . .
  - o We know it to be true about the theory of relativity that. . . .

  The strategy helps to highlight any unexamined assumptions that students are bringing to the class. As groups are determining their truth statements, or classmates are refuting those statements in the larger discussion, the "complexity and ambiguity" of knowledge is cast in sharp relief. This can productively lead to further study, paper and project topics, and conversations for the next class.
- Nonstructured scene setting: This strategy purposefully tries to minimize instructor moderation. Instead of giving directions for discussion, the instructor sets the scene with a collection of images, quotes from the reading, issues or phrases, names, or events. It could be a piece of music or video clip. The instructor then lets students know that they are to field the discussion among themselves for a particular amount of time. You might even tell students that it's difficult for you to stay out of the discussion and ask them to moderate your reactions, or you could give yourself the role of notetaker and wrap up the class with a summary of what students have uncovered through their discussion.

Engaging the *Whole* Class

What should you do when one student dominates class discussion? In F2F classes there are often one or two students who arrive eager, even intensely compelled to talk in class. Many of us have been that student. There are lots of reasons why certain students feel compelled (and entitled) to talk: an intense interest in the subject, a desire to please the teacher, fear of silence, an extroverted nature, or a strong feeling of entitlement in stating their opinions. While we might appreciate students who start the conversational ball rolling, be careful not to let the same students dominate class discussion. Ask yourself "Who is talking in my classroom? Are certain categories of students dominating while others silently observe?" (Howard, 2015, p. 68). The strength of a good discussion comes from hearing multiple points of view, not watching a dialogue between the instructor and one or two students. Once this dynamic occurs, other students often become quiet because they assume that the talkative student will take responsibility for responding or they may feel that their own perspectives are not valued (Howard, 2015).[2] Some students may be intimidated by the confidence and authority of these outgoing students. When Aeron was a freshman there was a very confident student who responded to the teacher's every question with enviable self-assurance. He was so articulate and fast on his feet that few other students found a way to enter the conversation. Aeron remembers being surprised when she found out that the quiet woman next to her earned the highest grade on the final, not the loquacious young man. It takes a while for students to realize that the person who talks the most is not necessarily the one with the most to contribute.

One easy solution is to use the prewriting and small group activities listed above to create smaller conversations with a rotating role for a group spokesperson. This helps students share the responsibility for contributing to class and allows you to demonstrate that you value and welcome a wide range of perspectives. This also gives quieter students a chance to vet their ideas and build confidence by articulating them in a smaller setting. If you still have one or two students who dominate the conversation despite your efforts, a diplomatic approach is to ask the talkative student to stay after class, privately thank them for their active participation, and then tell them that you don't want the other students in the class to become dependent on them and that class discussions are richer when more people talk. Students usually appreciate being taken into your confidence and being recognized as a strong contributor. This is also a good time to refer back to the established ground rules and ask the talkative student to practice leaning back and letting others speak first.

Checking In and Getting Feedback

Although most courses will ask students to fill out a student evaluation of your teaching at the end of the semester, that information comes too late to improve your teaching for that course. The good news is that you can ask students for their feedback in informal surveys at any point during the semester, and use that feedback to gauge how the course is going and to make adjustments, if necessary. There will be key moments throughout the term when you'll want to ask students for feedback about the course, typically after you've graded some major assignment. We often refer to this as mid-semester feedback, but it can be done at any point. The simplest approach is to ask students these five questions:

1. What are we doing in this course that is helping you to learn?
2. What are we doing that isn't helping you to learn?
3. What could be added to the course that would help you to learn better?
4. What are you doing in the course that's helping you to be successful?

5. What could you start doing that might help you to be more successful?

You can also include a couple of additional questions tailored to the specific course. For example, you might want to ask them if they find the course textbook helpful. Some other questions to consider include the following:

1. How well prepared were they to complete the major assignment?
2. What one activity, reading, or resource was most helpful to them?
3. Did your feedback help them understand what they need to do to improve their next assignment?
4. How effective were their own study and learning strategies?

If you set up these open lines of communication with your students, you will be able to better adjust your strategies. After you read through their feedback, summarize what you read and share it with them in class (or in an online course message). If you make changes in response to their feedback, let them know and be sure to keep your directions and due dates transparent. It's OK to say, "Hey, it looks like you're telling me that X isn't working and you'd prefer it if we tried Y. I hear you and here are the changes I've made." If students suggest a change that you aren't willing to make, use this opportunity to tell them why you are sticking with your original plan. Aeron routinely hears from roughly half of her class that small group work isn't helpful, but the other half of the class finds these groups very useful. When Aeron reports back to the class the results of the survey, she points this discrepancy out to them and explains that this is why she employs small groups for some of her classes but makes sure to employ other activities.

Notice that good surveys avoid questions about preferences, such as "What do you like about this course so far?" and instead focus on learning. The last two questions listed above also lead students to a more metacognitive understanding of their own ways of learning. Students' answers to these questions may give you a clue as to what additional resources they need to be successful. For example, if students are providing answers like "I would do better on the quizzes if I understood the mathematical terms," then maybe you could provide some optional online self-graded vocab quizzes for students. Or, if students say "I would have done better on this paper if I had gotten feedback earlier," then you could take time to connect students with the writing center and help them set up a consultation before the next paper is due. Your department or your campus's teaching and learning center may even have forms you can use for mid-semester feedback. One resource that we recommend is Brown's Sheridan Center for Teaching and Learning, which offers a variety of mid-semester surveys, including examples for small seminars, labs, and large courses.

Student Evaluations of Teaching

Most instructors get feedback from their students in the form of the official student evaluations of teaching done at the end of the semester. These surveys are anonymous, and the results typically aren't shared with an instructor until after the semester has ended. These surveys can provide valuable feedback that you can use to revise your course the next time you teach it. However, they do little to help you improve the course as you are teaching it and can be unfairly used as the sole factor in judging an instructor's teaching ability. Don't get us wrong, feedback from your students, even after the course has ended, provides useful information, but we encourage you to use students' comments as "formative" feedback and not as a judgement of your teaching effectiveness. (See Chapter 7 for an overview of the research indicating bias in student evaluations of teaching.)

Reading students' evaluations of your teaching can be fascinating, but it can also be unsettling, especially when students comment on aspects of your personality or appearance. Aeron remembers when a good friend read this student comment: "The textbook is boring, his lectures are boring, and even his hair is boring." This happens more often to women and minoritized instructors. Students may also use evaluations as an opportunity to vent their frustration over the textbook, the course requirements, or even the time of day the course was offered—all things legitimately out of your control. A graduate student who had won a prestigious university-wide teaching award admitted that he routinely gets at least one very negative comment from a student on each of his final course evaluations. "Unless it's constructive and points out a specific aspect of the course that the student felt wasn't useful, then I ignore the comment" (José, Linguistics). Not all of us are as thick-skinned, particularly when we begin teaching. And even tenured faculty routinely express their dismay at receiving negative comments. We all have a tendency to focus on negative feedback, or that one mean-spirited comment, instead of looking at the general trend and savoring the positive comments. Here are some strategies that can help you to use student feedback from final course evaluations in a constructive way:

1. If your campus uses electronic course evaluations, still give your F2F students designated time in class to complete

them. This will increase your response rate, which will give you a more accurate picture of your students' experiences.

2. Tell your students why their comments are important. Assure them that you won't be able to access the evaluations until after the grades are in, but also let them know that you will read their comments carefully and use their feedback to improve future courses.
3. Ask a friend or graduate student colleague to read through your evals and give you a summary. It's easier to be objective about someone else's evaluations.
4. Read through your comments once, noting any constructive suggestions and highlighting the appreciative remarks. When you read a negative comment, ask yourself, is this student pointing out something that I can improve? If so, note the improvement that you intend to make, but don't note the negative way it was phrased.
5. If you read a negative comment that isn't constructive, tell yourself that this student is most likely very frustrated and taking it out on you and then do your best to move on.
6. If you read several similar negative comments (such as "the instructor was hostile" or "his grading was unfair") take note. There may be something worth exploring here. Consider talking to a trusted colleague or your mentor or making a confidential appointment with someone in your teaching center to talk through ways you might address this.
7. When students give you positive feedback, let it sink in. Take notes or print out these comments and keep them in a file to use in your teaching statement, in an application for a teaching award, or to read when you feel discouraged.
8. If your university has a teaching center, make a confidential appointment with a staff member there and ask them to help you interpret and respond constructively to your student evaluations. Teaching center staff often have seen teaching

and student evaluations across disciplines and can help you put your evaluations into perspective and work with you to create a tangible plan for addressing issues of concern.

The best way to avoid nasty surprises when reading student evaluations is to create more opportunities for students to give you feedback throughout the semester. Conducting the kind of mid-semester feedback surveys we mention above will allow you to address issues before they develop into lasting complaints and before they become part of an official record of your teaching. In any case, remember that all of us, even those who have received awards for our teaching, have received negative comments on student evaluations.

Helping Your Students Study Smarter

The mid-semester feedback you receive from students might clue you in to what strategies are working for their learning and what strategies aren't. We can help students produce higher quality work by letting them know that there are more productive ways to study and structuring our courses to encourage this kind of behavior. Students often bring to college unproductive ways of studying and writing that don't align with research about how people learn. Let's picture a typical scenario: students listen to a lecture (either in person or online), read their textbooks with a highlighter in hand, and then cram the night before a midterm or exam. Sound familiar? According to recent work in the neuroscience of learning, this might be the *least effective* way to learn, so why would we structure our classes in ways that encourage this behavior?

Although not all the research can translate tidily into study strategies, experts agree that in order to remember something, it helps when we give students opportunities to *retrieve* or bring forth the information from their memories (Brown, Roediger, & McDaniel, 2018). This is also referred to as the "testing effect," although it's important to distinguish whether you're testing students for a grade or to help them learn. To put it simply, students learn more when they struggle to remember something (self-quizzing, using flashcards, or by writing) than when rereading a text or reviewing notes. What's troublesome is that the least effective study strategies often feel more successful—partly because they require less effort. However, it is precisely the struggle to recall something when you don't have it in front of you that creates more lasting memory. For example, have you ever been asked by a friend or child to define a word? You're familiar with the word, you've heard it before, but you may struggle when asked to give an accurate definition. Similarly, when we hear a lecture or reread material, we think that because it makes sense in the moment, or seems familiar, that we understand it. This is referred to as the "illusions of knowing" (Brown, Roediger, & McDaniel, 2018). Students would be better served if instead of rereading books and notes they took several short (low stakes) quizzes on the material or struggled to write down or verbalize a concept.[3]

Another way for students to level-up their memory and understanding is to interleave their studying:

> ***Interleaving*** boosts learning by mixing up closely related topics, which encourages students to develop the ability to distinguish between multiple concepts. For example, learning increases when students practice addition, subtraction, multiplication and division problems all mixed up, rather than one type of problem at a time (Agarwal, n.d.).

Like a tougher brain workout, this helps students strengthen their understanding and associations with the information they are trying to learn by differentiating it from other information. It's one thing to list contributing factors to the Cold War straight from the textbook, but it's harder for your brain to put that list into a developed argument explaining what actions the United States should or should not have taken regarding the Bay of Pigs.

Retrieving and interleaving are more taxing than simply reviewing material because our brains are working harder to access information outside of its expected context. The effort involved shows that you are learning. Students, however, may resist this type of studying at first because they assume that more effortful studying means they are doing something wrong. To help students practice and recognize when they are learning, try to include these strategies:

- Ask students to retrieve information in short, ungraded writing tasks.
- Give students more frequent, low-stakes assignments (not all of which must be graded).
- Ask students to make connections to earlier material throughout the semester.
- Make sure that exams or large projects are cumulative so students can apply their earlier learning.
- Consider assigning presentations or other opportunities for students to explain material to their classmates.
- Tell students about these more effective study strategies.[4]

Celebrating Progress

Take a ceremonial approach to the close of your course to help you and your students mark the progress you've made. "Conclusions are so important," argues Psychology Professor

R.A. Gurung, winner of the American Psychological Foundation Charles L. Brewer Distinguished Teaching of Psychology Award. Professor Gurung credits a course he took as an undergraduate on endings with informing his own approach to the last day of class. The course discussed major endings like death, leaving jobs, leaving college, or divorce and shaped the way he thinks of his semester:

> It taught me about the complex emotions involved in endings. During a semester, I get attached to the cohort of students and experience sadness. In my Introduction to Psychology course, I put as much attention into my last class as I do my first class: *every minute is scripted*. After finishing whatever content is left and doing a review for the final, I end in a crescendo, an impassioned speech focused on what I most want them to remember from the semester. I challenge myself by asking, what are the handful of things I want students to remember 20 years from now? I recap our course goals from the first day and point out what we did to reach those goals. And, I end with an explicit and sincere invitation to them to stay connected. (R. A. Gerung, personal communication, February 17, 2021)

You might revisit some of the goals students set on the first day, or the gains they've made. You could also put together a highlight reel (screenshots or even a video) that celebrates the strong work students have tackled over the term. If you plan to ask students what they learned or about their changes over the course of the semester, be prepared to share an account of your own growth. And, lastly, thank your students for their time, for the energy they put into the course, and for trusting you to help them learn. It's a big deal for many students to complete a college course. By celebrating this achievement, you are holding space for them to feel that sense of pride and accomplishment.

Planning Meets Practice

Your careful planning of each class or module conveys to your students that you are a committed instructor and helps you to be more confident in your teaching. Thinking through different classroom scenarios ahead of time allows you to respond with more confidence in the moment. It's hard work, but the payoff is a class that is well structured and where your students feel that their time and contributions have been valued. You might hear colleagues or your advisors comment about how little they prepare to teach. This is much like students admitting how little they have read or studied. Both cases might be defense mechanisms used to deflect responsibility for a potentially poor outcome. If you catch yourself participating in this dismissive attitude, maybe ask yourself why you would be afraid of caring *too* much about doing a good job teaching?

Of course, even with all your planning and forethought you will still find yourself surprised when something doesn't unfold the way you anticipated. This happens to even the most experienced educators, but it's often more common when you begin teaching. This can be a great time to develop a reflective practice. At the end of each unit, module, or week jot down in a notebook or even on the syllabus itself what worked and what didn't. You often have so many ideas about what worked or didn't work in the moment, but it's easy to forget them when you prepare to teach the course again. Some challenges may leave you bewildered and wondering how to respond. In the next chapter, we'll help you think about how to navigate some of the more challenging teaching scenarios.

KEY TAKEAWAYS

- Create an outline for in-person teaching to keep you on track.
- Check in with students to see how the course is going while there is still time for you to make adjustments or add resources.
- Take notes as you go through the semester so you remember what small tweaks to make the next time. Even the best laid plans might benefit from revisions.

CHAPTER 5

NAVIGATING CLASSROOM CHALLENGES

Things can go wrong despite your careful planning. Often, we have no idea why some students check-out of a class—refusing to participate, missing class, or coming late. Aeron once taught a seemingly confident, outgoing male student who began to miss class and when he was present he expressed a growing cynicism toward class material. Because he had a strong voice, his negative attitude affected class discussions and sometimes made Aeron defensive. Later in the semester she learned that he was a combat veteran who suffered from PTSD and he had been temporarily homeless. Since then, Aeron has read more about veterans' experiences in college and has come to understand how many aspects of the classroom environment may be challenging for them (Wright, 2016). Despite all the interventions and sound strategies we've provided thus far, each class has a chemistry that is impacted by the overall class dynamic and the unique circumstances of individual students. There are factors affecting individual students that make it difficult for them to focus on the material and become part of the classroom community and which could prevent them from feeling like they belong in your classroom.

For example, students are less able to pay attention when they are tired, distracted, or coping with trauma. We all only have so much cognitive energy, and disruptions in students' lives deplete this energy. Cia Verschelden's meta-analysis across several health and social science studies demonstrates the deleterious effects on physical and mental health caused by systemic racism, poverty, and social marginalization (Verschelden, 2017). Moreover, inequitable access to healthcare and resources often exacerbates these issues when individuals do struggle. This is important to remember when you start to hear your advisors or mentors describe students as "underprepared" or "at risk." Students' abilities to thrive in any learning environment are deeply entangled with the cognitive resources that they can dedicate to their learning as opposed to their job, their mental or physical health, their caretaking responsibilities, or the safety and welfare of their family and community.

Anxiety, for example, is one of the most common emotions experienced during learning and you might be surprised at the ways your students cope with it. Whereas some anxiety can help people pay attention and learn, too much anxiety is counterproductive (Cavanagh, 2016). Undergraduate students face unprecedented levels of anxiety and may often try to self-regulate their anxiety by procrastinating. Procrastination is often a way to regulate negative emotions associated with performance anxiety ("I suck at writing"; "I'm never going to be able to complete this project on time"; "Everyone else gets it, but I don't"). You might be thinking, doesn't procrastination lead to more stressful situations or poorer grades? It can, but it also allows students to create a protective barrier between their sense of self and the grade they get on an assignment. If you procrastinate and only spend one night writing a major paper then the grade reflects that compromised effort, and the student can avoid some of their anxieties. Again, you are not your students' therapist, but it might help to understand that some students engage in counterproductive behavior because they are attempting to regulate their moods, not necessarily because they are unmotivated or don't value your class (Lieberman, 2019).

Stereotype Threat

Feelings of self-doubt and isolation may cause students from underrepresented groups additional risk. They may experience something called *stereotype threat*: the fear of confirming a negative stereotype about an aspect of one's identity. This creates an added mental tax on students. Claude Steele and Joshua Aronson (1995) conducted studies with undergraduates and found that Black students underperformed on tests in which they were aware of a stereotype that expected them to underperform. Similarly, women underperformed on math tests when they were given the impression that the test measured gender difference but performed well when the test was described as gender neutral (Spencer, Steele, & Quinn, 1999). Steele's explanation is that being reminded of society's prejudices—that women are bad at math or that Black students underperform academically—creates an apprehension and fear that adds to students' cognitive load and causes them to do worse (Steele & Aronson, 1995). While anyone could experience some type of stereotype threat, certain groups of students are more at risk. Multiple studies have found that stereotype threat significantly reduces performance for undergraduates from less privileged socioeconomic statuses (Croizet & Claire, 1998), Black students

(Steele & Aronson, 1995), women (Good, Aronson, & Harder, 2008), Latinx students (Schmader & Johns, 2003), and LGBTQ students at traditionally religious institutions (Love, 1998). Without careful thought about how best to structure your course, you may inadvertently set up some students to disengage and increase their likelihood of failing.

Growth Mindset

One way to combat stereotype threats in your classroom is by cultivating a growth mindset within your students. Growth mindset strategies appear throughout the literature as a way to help students recognize challenges as learning opportunities and to see themselves as capable of building new skills and expertise. Having a growth mindset is believing that effort combined with effective learning strategies and resources will result in learning—and not seeing missteps as a personal reflection of one's limited abilities. When learning isn't happening, then an individual with a growth mindset recognizes that they need to adjust either their effort or their strategy. Steve Stroessner and Catherine Good have developed several research-based strategies based on the concepts of growth mindset specifically aimed at mitigating the negative effects of stereotype threat in the classroom:

- "Emphasize the importance of effort and motivation in performance while de-emphasizing inherent talent or genius.
- Emphasize high standards with assurances about [students'] capability for meeting them.
- Encourage individuals to think of themselves as complex and multifaceted.

- Offer individuals explanations for why anxiety and distraction are occurring that do not implicate the self or validate the stereotype." (Stroessner & Good as cited in Rhys, n.d.)

It's helpful to remind students that their brains function like muscles that will respond to strategic effort and encourage them to seek help or try new strategies or resources when their efforts don't seem to be yielding results (Yaeger et al., 2019). Carol Dweck, the researcher credited with initiating this body of research, cautions educators not to oversimplify the growth mindset to simply encourage students to try harder, or praise any effort (Dweck, 2016). Students who are trying tremendously hard, but still not seeing any learning gains, may feel defeated thinking that all their effort hasn't been worthwhile. In an interview with *The Atlantic*, Dweck clarifies, "Students need to know that if they're stuck, they don't just need effort. You don't want them redoubling their efforts with the same ineffective strategies. You want them to know when to ask for help and when to use resources that are available" (Gross-Loh, 2016).

Students are also sensitive to whether we, as instructors, believe that they can succeed with the right strategies and effort. When we presume that certain students will fail our courses no matter what, that message comes across loud and clear. Think of the old first-day threat: "Look to your right and to your left, only half of you will pass this class." Our attitudes toward students and our assumptions about their intelligence can exacerbate systemic challenges already present in the classroom. A recent study conducted with 150 STEM faculty and 15,000 students shows that instructors who have a "fixed" mindset, who believe that a student's intelligence and ability to succeed in the class is already determined, engender less motivation in students than those instructors who have a growth mindset or a belief that well-directed effort can result in better performance and understanding (Canning et al., 2019). Particularly alarming is the finding that in classes where instructors have fixed mindsets, *there are larger racial achievement gaps* (Canning et al., 2019). While we may not intentionally communicate these attitudes, or even realize that we hold them, our beliefs about students' capabilities are expressed in how we structure assignments, grade, and even who we call on in class. Ideally, we would assume that every student in our class, with effort and proper support, can achieve success and we would structure our classroom accordingly. In addition, it's important that you not assume that a student's challenges are a result of a lack of effort on their part. Systemic racism, poverty, and mental and physical health challenges all impact your students' lives and the effort you are perceiving may not be a realistic reflection of the effort they are putting in to be a part of your course.

Responding to Disruptions

A different kind of classroom challenge can come from disruptions to your teaching. As faculty developers, we've had an increasing number of faculty and graduate teaching assistants come to us for support on what they perceive as problematic student behaviors that frustrate, disrupt, and sometimes, in rare cases, genuinely frighten instructors. As early as 1996, Robert Boice noted from classroom observations that "classroom incivilities" are widespread in college courses but are rarely discussed. He includes within his definition of *incivility* a range of behaviors that include both student and instructor behavior: "(1) Teachers displaying aloof, distancing mannerisms; (2) teachers discouraging student involvement with fast-paced lectures; (3) students' noisiness and indifference; (4) students coming late and leaving early; (5) students' sarcastic remarks/gestures" (Boice, 1996). Since 1996, with the atmosphere of increased political hostility and the rare but troubling cases of campus mass violence, and the increased reporting of campus sexual assault, instructors have become more attuned to the possibilities of threat in their classrooms. However, it is important to distinguish between student behavior that can be defined as *rude, disruptive,* or *hostile.* Since these terms are often used interchangeably but don't necessarily have the same impact, it's helpful to define what we mean in each case before we strategize how to prevent and address these behaviors.

In the first category is student behavior that seems disrespectful or *rude*: For example, a student who leaves class in the middle of a discussion, checks their cell phone, or who falls asleep in class. These are examples of behaviors that might be irritating to you, but they may have very innocent causes, such as medical issues or working a late shift. They could be because of cultural differences, and probably are not meant to be disrespectful. As an undergraduate, Stephanie once saw an instructor refuse to let a student re-enter the classroom after he had stepped outside to blow his nose and grab a drink of water from the water fountain. The instructor said it was rude to leave and come back during his lecture, and the student countered that it would have been rude for him to blow his nose loudly during class. For these minor issues, we encourage you to let it go or speak to the student privately. You can also avoid several of these standoffs by not adopting policies that cause undue physical restraints on students in the classroom; sometimes folks simply do need to get up and use the bathroom. Students appreciate being given the same benefit of the doubt that you would give any adult or colleague. However you decide to address these relatively minor behaviors, we encourage you to assume that they are not personal.

The second category of student behaviors is trickier: students who *disrupt* the classroom in a way that makes it difficult for you to do your job and for other students to learn. For example, a student who continues to challenge you about a grade during class or students who are loudly having a side conversation. Don't ignore these kinds of behaviors since they also risk frustrating other students. Instead, we recommend that you calmly address the behavior either immediately or privately after class. In either scenario, begin by asking questions to see if there is something that you are unaware of (Race & Pickford, 2007).

Late in the semester, in a large survey course, Stephanie was trying to get class started when a student began questioning the courses grading scheme. What started with a quick question before class, quickly devolved into the student loudly complaining about how unfair she found some of the required class activities. Other students were starting a reading quiz, but still the student continued to voice her opinion across the room. Hoping the student would calm down, Stephanie let this go on for a few moments before she realized how disruptive this was to the other 45 students who were trying to complete their quizzes. She decided she needed to do something. So, she moved closer to the student, let her know that it was time to begin the day's classwork, that her comments were making it hard for her peers to work, and offered to continue the conversation after class to allow the student more time to explain her concerns. Whether it was the pressure of being addressed directly or having the behavior described as disruptive, this was enough to quiet the student and allow the class to progress. While the student was clearly unhappy during class, she was no longer speaking loudly and off topic while others were trying to work. When Stephanie followed up with the student after class, it became clear that the student was concerned about her overall grade in the course and how she could raise it. Stephanie discussed what options the student had at that point in the term to make a difference in her grade. This didn't excuse the disruptive behavior, though, so Stephanie told her the behavior seemed out of character and asked what was going on. At this comment, the student became more introspective and admitted that she was also not proud of how she had behaved. It was the end of the term, she was carrying a full load, and she was getting anxious about her final grades in all her classes.

Often, students don't realize that they are being disruptive—whether it's because they are too wrapped up in their own experiences or because they simply aren't paying attention to their surroundings. When deciding what to do next, you might ask the student or the class to weigh in. If it feels relevant to address the disruption in the moment, you might learn something about how your entire class is feeling but only a few are expressing. For example, if a student is contesting the fairness of an exam question you might learn that the rest of the class also felt confused by the same question. When you determine what the next step is, be sure to take the action and follow up with the student(s) with whom you spoke. Document the interaction and the results so that you can use it as an example when setting expectations with future classes (this documentation can be as simple as sending yourself an email). If a student continues to be disruptive despite your conversation, this documentation can also help you accurately talk about patterns of behavior with your department leadership and other teaching mentors in order to ask for resources.

When you ask students honest questions about what they may be going through, you may receive information you weren't prepared for. Stephanie remembers one day, after class, asking a student who was consistently showing up late to her course what was going on. The class heavily relied on group work, and she had to disrupt at least one group's activities each time to get him situated. When she asked him what was causing lateness, he lowered his voice and turned his body so other students who were still in the classroom couldn't hear his response. His electricity had been shut off, which meant he didn't have a reliable alarm to wake him up; he took the bus to campus, so missing one bus dramatically impacted when he arrived at campus. At that exact moment, Stephanie didn't know what she could do for this student beyond being better prepared to get him situated in the class's activities the next time he arrived late. Today, she would have asked the student if she could connect him to student services and local resources that might have helped him with his utility bills. Make yourself aware of your campus and local community resources that help people in need. If you teach F2F, keep cards, brochures, and fliers on hand in your teaching materials. If you teach online or maintain an online presence for your course, be sure to include these resources prominently along with explanations of how they can help students. Sometimes students won't share their challenges directly, like the student in Stephanie's class, but they might start showing up late, having more absences, or falling asleep in class. Reach out to these students or approach them after class to express your concern and see if they are OK. Students frequently don't realize the extent to which their instructors do care about their well-being. You also might be the only person that interacts with that student and asks if they are doing ok.

Unfortunately, there are times when the classroom can become a *hostile* place. The pageantry of overheated discussions are so common in cable news and in social media that students might not recognize when they are creating a hostile environment for one another. If you know that you'll be discussing a charged topic in class, review your co-created list of shared expectations for class interactions together before the discussion begins; remind students what they have committed to, and encourage them to recognize the difference between their discomfort at encountering something new and being the subject of a threatening act or speech. Hostile behavior that poses a threat can look like the following:

- A student violates your personal space.
- A student raises their voice and seems irrational.
- A student implies or makes a direct threat to harm themselves or others.
- A student displays a firearm or weapon.
- A student physically confronts or attacks another student.
- A student stalks or harasses an instructor (University of Oregon Counseling Services, n.d.).

If you experience any of these behaviors, dismiss the class and/or call campus security. It's okay to swiftly end class or remove yourself from an environment that does not feel safe. It's also okay to tell your students at the beginning of the semester that this is what you will do should you see threatening behavior in the classroom.

Often we're not sure how to interpret a student's behavior. Sakura, a graduate student, recalled a student in her Japanese class whose behavior become increasingly troubling: "At first, he was just annoying. He positioned himself as superior to everyone else in the class. Then his behavior become more alarming: posting semi-naked anime pictures on the discussion board and then writing about killing someone in his language assignment. I didn't know what was going on with him; was he having some sort of a mental health crisis? [sic] I had no idea what to do." Eventually Sakura reached out to the dean of students as well as the campus student mental health center. Many graduate students aren't given guidelines on how to interpret or respond to this type of behavior. This might feel scary to think about, but we want you to be prepared and realize that you and your students deserve to feel safe in your classroom. Reach out to one of your mentors to get their advice and support if you are experiencing what seems like disruptive or hostile behavior.

As you continue teaching, you'll discover that each class is radically new, no matter how many times you've taught it. Each time you encounter a new group of students, a relationship develops, not just between you and each student, but, hopefully, among the students themselves. The unique aspects of each class are why the same material that sparked an amazing discussion last semester may fall flat the second time you teach it. If you teach multiple sections of the same course, you will probably notice that one section just gels better or seems more engaged, whereas a second section of the same course may feel flat, disengaged, and just suck the energy out of you. Class dynamics can also be affected by environmental constraints out of your control, such as the assigned classroom, the meeting time, or the online learning management system. Your own energy levels and mood can affect the class dynamics as well. A disengaged class can be revived and a class that began as lively can run out of steam if not engaged. What happens in an actual course or discussion section is always bigger than the sum of its parts. Put another way, the exact same syllabus, assignments, and learning outcomes can produce radically different experiences—for you and for your students. Over time you'll learn how to calibrate these strategies to build the right kind of community for each of your courses.

KEY TAKEAWAYS

- Students face a variety of challenges that aren't always evident and that may affect their performance in class.
- Students may exhibit behavior that is rude, disruptive, or even threatening. Plan to reduce the likelihood of these behaviors, but also be aware of your campus resources in case the behaviors occur.

CHAPTER 6

CREATING ASSIGNMENTS AND RESPONDING TO STUDENT WORK

Grading is everyone's least favorite part of teaching. Each of us has spent hours bleary-eyed with a *slooowly* shrinking stack of student papers while drinking countless cups of caffeine. Aeron remembers calculating how many more papers she could grade before midnight, then getting so tired that she started calculating how many she could grade if she woke up at 5:00 a.m. Stephanie would pile students' papers beside her bed and not allow herself out of her room on the weekends until she had made it through the stack. Neither of these are great ideas. Why is grading so onerous? After all, responding to student work is an opportunity to see students' thinking made visible and to give them valuable feedback. But it can be tedious when we make the same corrections over and over. It's disheartening when your students haven't grasped the material that you've worked so hard to teach them. When we care deeply about the topics we are teaching, poor student work can seem intentionally sloppy or even feel like a lack of appreciation for the subject or you. In addition, when students are socialized to see grades as their primary goal, grades can become the site of many power struggles. It's stressful to be challenged over a grade when you're a graduate teaching assistant and have little institutional authority. One of the reasons grading can be so taxing is that instructors and students often are working with bad information on how to learn and how to assess learning. In this chapter, we will help you create assignments that align with your learning goals and give the greatest possibility of bringing forth strong student work. While there is no magic trick that will eliminate the time and effort it takes to respond to student work, careful assignment design and feedback can help make responding to student work more satisfying for you *and* for them.

Creating Assignments

One of the best ways to receive better student work is to design better assignments. If you have the freedom to construct the course yourself, or to significantly modify the course, we suggest you begin by continuing the work you did in Chapter 2. What skills and lasting understandings do you want students to retain after the course is over? Assignments are *student thinking made visible,* or a performance of their understanding. It's easy to assume students understand the material you cover because, well, it makes sense to you! However, just because you cover material does not mean that students understand it or that they will remember it. We often fool ourselves (and students fool themselves) into thinking that passively absorbing information is deep and lasting understanding. Online and blended courses help to alleviate this tracking problem because online students can't appear to understand the material by smiling and nodding: they must formulate and record their thoughts, which makes it easier to see where/when students struggle. In online courses, students often participate by writing or uploading videos. When students *perform* their understanding, you can gauge if they are learning and examine the progress of the whole class.

Students can demonstrate their understanding in two ways: summative assignments and formative assignments. *Summative assignments* show the most polished version of students' thinking or progress and these are often weighted heavily to demonstrate their importance. For example, a research paper, a final exam, a presentation, a portfolio, or perhaps a course project can all serve as summative assignments. *Formative assignments* are the smaller activities or assignments that help students gain the skills necessary to produce these larger works or perform well on a major exam. Formative assignments should be either ungraded or worth a smaller percentage of the final grade. Formative assignments build in opportunities for students to practice the skills they will need, with several short papers or quizzes, so that if they don't master the skill the first time, they have a chance to get feedback and do better. Table 4 shows some examples of larger, summative assignments and the smaller formative assignments that scaffold or build up to major projects.

Table 4 Summative and Formative Assignments

Summative Assignments	Formative Assignments for Scaffolding
Longer research papers	In-class writing Short response papers Annotated bibliographies or literature reviews Paper proposals Rough drafts
Midterm or final exams	Short quizzes Clicker questions or polls Group practice exams In-class writing or problem solving
Presentations or projects	Think-pair-share Concept maps Journals Small group work

Breaking Down the Steps of an Assignment

What we have done in Table 4 is to break down the skills needed for a large assignment into smaller, component parts, which is called *scaffolding*. Scaffolding allows students to show their learning and also shows where they struggle. For example, if you require students to write a research paper, first give them an example of an annotated bibliography and explain its purpose, then ask them to write one. Next, have them write a proposal that outlines their tentative argument and give them feedback on it. They might then present their research to the whole class or to a partner before they write their final paper. If you are able, allow students to revise their final papers based on your feedback. Each component described above can be worth a small percentage of their grade, which grows proportionally during the semester. The early annotated bibliography and drafts may be worth a small amount, and the final draft or revisions would be worth more. The advantage of breaking larger projects into smaller assignments is that it creates conditions where all students can realistically end up with a satisfactory final paper. It also curtails student procrastination, reveals where students are struggling, helps to yield better work, and minimizes the temptations for academic dishonesty. If this sounds like a lot of work, it is. However, final papers will be better and less frustrating to grade.

When scaffolding to a larger assignment, tell students how each smaller assignment will prepare them for the larger assignment and the learning goals for the course. Students resent what they perceive to be busy work as much as you likely do. Show them a model or example of the assignment, preferably a paper or project completed by a former student. Aeron likes to use two solid-but-not-spectacular examples of student work so that students aren't intimidated and so that they don't assume that there is only one correct way to complete the assignment. If you don't have any student examples yet, consider what work from your own college classes you'd be willing to share. In introductory writing courses, Stephanie asks students to critique one of her early undergraduate essays—essays that have all the signs of a beginning college writer. The exercise allows the students to position themselves as experts and helps Stephanie make the point that learning to develop one's academic voice is a process. Take some time to discuss your assignment directions, the examples or models, and the ways that you will evaluate student work (this last component is called a *rubric*, which we will discuss more below). Here are some examples of low-stakes formative assignments that can help students build the skills and understanding they will need to complete longer work:

- Minute papers: Ask students to reflect, in writing, on a question at the start of class. For example, if students have been assigned to read an excerpt from Marx's *Capital*, ask them to briefly define "use value" and "exchange value" and to give an example from their own lives when an object's use value had no relation to its exchange value.
- Muddiest point papers: Ask students to comment on what is still unclear to them at the end of class or end of a unit. For example, at the end of a class discussion in a psychology course, ask each student to reflect on what is still unclear to them about Maslow's hierarchy of needs.
- Concept maps: Ask students to draw a visual representation of their understanding. For example, ask students to draw their understanding of the stages of cellular respiration, map thematic categories for 20th century artists and examples of their respective movements, or create a table that compares different philosophical approaches to big-picture questions.
- Feedback on paper drafts: Give students feedback on either rough drafts turned into the instructor or have them review each other's drafts in class.
- Verbal feedback: Discuss students' ideas with them before they draft their papers. This can be done in a student-instructor conference or a short video response.
- Low-stakes quizzes: Create quizzes that can be retaken until a student receives a passing grade. These can be built in your university learning management system and automatically graded to help you save time. If you build in explanations for incorrect answers, this can be a real benefit to students when they are learning.

Make sure to explain how you will assess these low-stakes assignments. We recommend not correcting them, but instead allowing students to compare their answers for accuracy in pairs or groups. If you are worried that students won't take these formative ungraded assignments seriously, give each assignment a check mark, which together will count for an overall percentage of their final grade. If a student's exercise shows no evidence of them having read the material or understood the assignment, you can give it a check minus: this also allows you to catch struggling students early on. Make it clear that students' writing in these informal, low-stakes assignments will not be corrected; rather, these exercises are meant to help them develop their ideas. Since you will not be grading these assignments (other than based on completion), they will take very little of your time and students can focus on formulating their ideas instead of sounding smart or regurgitating the textbook. Ungraded feedback can also give you a sense of where students are struggling, and what material you might need to explain further.

Choice and Flexibility in Assignments

When Jonathan, a biology graduate student, was teaching a course on animal behavior he realized that giving students choices on how they addressed the topic gave them greater motivation and engagement with the material. For example, in a unit on the great Serengeti migration he asked students to pick a specific endemic Serengeti animal (such as the African elephant, giraffe, zebra, gazelle, wildebeest, buffalo, ostrich, vulture, warthog, Nile crocodile, spotted hyena, etc.) and to use their chosen animal to discuss how animals participate in variant seasonal migrations. This assignment required students to research their answers and cite multiple primary sources. The specificity and creativity of his assignment—his guiding questions about tracking versus territoriality, natal dispersal, heard symbionts, and migration causation—engaged students by allowing them to focus on what was most interesting to them about the topic.

Erin, an MFA student in the art department, was assigned to teach a required course on shop foundations. The original assignment was to create a toolbox in plywood using woodshop tools and techniques and a box in steel using metal shop tools and techniques. Although she understood the importance of students being taught to safely use the equipment, she noticed that art students found this assignment uninspiring, and she didn't blame them: in her mind this was a missed opportunity for students to practice making art. The next time she taught the course she decided to tailor the assignment to allow for more creativity while maintaining the same learning outcome: that students become competent in using the equipment and using it safely. She revised the assignment so that instead of making simple boxes, students could create art that was meaningful to them. For this project, students created abstract geometric sculptures, a mobile of steel stars, an alien figure that rocked on a rounded bottom, and a heavy metal crown. "It felt important to allow them more freedom to play and make something that really excited them, rather than focus on a particular outcome. My hope was that this would encourage them to continue to want to work with metal in more advanced sculpture courses," Erin explained.

In both of these examples graduate student teachers kept their departmental student learning outcomes but created assignments that allowed their students more choice and autonomy. As we discussed in Chapter 3, students are more motivated when they have some measure of control or choice in their work (Pekrun, 2006). In addition to allowing students choices, the revised assignments projected more of the instructors' own enthusiasm and commitment to teaching. Are there places in your course assignments where you could allow students more choices?

In addition to offering choices, allowing students some measure of flexibility in completing their work shows students that you respect them and emphasizes their ability to master the learning objectives, rather than following rules. One of Aeron's teaching mentors is Professor Alicia F. Chávez, author of *Teaching Across Cultural Strengths*. In her workshops, Dr. Chávez stresses creating "multiple on-ramps" for students to achieve excellence, explaining, "I teach future teachers and our state needs them and needs them to be excellent. I am committed to supporting them and giving them flexibility so achieve this." What might this flexibility look like in your own course? Consider these ideas:

- Accept some late work. For example, you might issue every student a "pass" that allows them to hand in an assignment one week late. This acknowledges that students have complicated lives, places you outside of the role of excuse cop, and recognizes the inequity that occurs when more privileged students feel more comfortable asking for lenience. (Make sure that you make this policy clear at the beginning of the semester in your syllabus.)
- Give students multiple ways to master the course material. Are you measuring students' knowledge through tests alone, or with papers only? Using one form of assessment unfairly rewards students who are good at test taking or who are already strong writers. Consider allowing students to show you that they've mastered the material by other means, such as presentations or projects.

- Allow students to retake quizzes or exams and use the highest grade instead of an average. This rewards mastery over initial preparedness.

Below are some examples of other ways to assess your students' learning. In each of these examples, instructors developed creative tasks that require students to do more than cram information for a test or produce an academic analysis:

- Wikis: Class webpages where students work collaboratively to create a public document, such as terms for the course.
- Interviews: Creating primary sources from peers or community members. For example, students could interview community members about historical events they experienced, such as the Holocaust, WWII, or civil rights activities in their region.
- Posters: In courses where students engage in undergraduate research, final projects can be posters in the style of the discipline.
- Mini conferences: Students in the class present their final work in panels.
- Portfolios: Students revise and collect their most polished work from the class.
- Lesson plans: Students develop structured ways that they might teach a particular topic to other students or younger learners.
- Infographics: Students make sense of complex data with eye-catching visualizations.
- Podcasts: Students create audio projects to tell a story, make an argument, or present research.
- Brochures: Students could produce advertising material for community partners or hypothetical audiences. For example,

technical writing students work with community organizations to create informational brochures.

- Editorials: Students are asked to formulate arguments about topical course content in the form of a newspaper editorial.
- Debate: Students use evidence and research from the course to engage in a structured argument.
- Blogs: Students create public, intellectual content for a lay audience.
- Dramatization or role play: Students are assigned roles to reenact or respond to moments in history or literature. There is a national history teaching initiative pioneered by Barnard College Professor Mark Carnes, "reacting to the past," which offers structured guides that can be used to teach a variety of historical topics.
- Projects or "UnEssays": These are creative final projects (in place of a traditional research paper) in which students engage in course content and conduct research. Often, students are allowed to choose their medium (blog, art project game, etc.), submit a proposal, and produce a written reflection of their learning. For example, a student in Aeron's British novels class researched 19th century British cuisine and prepared a class meal that allowed her to discuss colonialism, British domestic culture, and gender roles.[1]

Creating Authentic Assignments

Authentic assessments are assignments that more closely mirror the types of work that practitioners in the field or discipline might do. For example, instead of a formal research paper debunking learning styles in an education course, ask students to draft a memo to high school teachers explaining that new research suggests people do not have one "style" of learning. In a biology course, you might have students create blog reviews of two selected websites to point out how each one models scientific literacy. Students often put more effort into projects where the audience isn't just the professor since professors already know the material and therefore students aren't informing you of something new. In fact, students may assume that professors read their work only to mark what is wrong. However, constructing projects for community partners or peers who need the student's limited expertise or skills gives students a greater and more authentic sense of purpose. If you don't have an outside audience for your students, consider creating hypothetical audiences. For example, if you are teaching introduction to American history, ask students to analyze several conflicting primary sources about public statues and write an editorial for a local newspaper explaining their analysis. Authentic assignments can better motivate your students, can be tailored to your students' capabilities and interests, can de-incentivize cheating, and will be more engaging to grade. They are also wonderful opportunities for students to try on disciplinary ways of thinking.

Here are some specific examples of authentic assignments from faculty in different disciplines and across institutions:

> **Education:** At Indiana University, Professor Joshua Danish asks his educational psychology students to apply the cognitive theories they have learned to interpret children's behaviors. Students record detailed observations of elementary school pupils' learning and post them online. Other students are then asked to apply specific theories to these descriptions of learning. Through this exercise, students improve their ability to describe learning in detail and they are able to connect abstract theories of learning to concrete examples (2012).

Foreign languages: Linguistics Professor Alwiya Omar helps her students learn Swahili by engaging in an activity with strong roots in African languages and cultures: storytelling. Students write, in Swahili, a series of stories about their own experiences or current events and post them to a class wiki, where they receive feedback from their classmates. At the end of the semester, students publish their revised stories in podcasts (2012).

Biology: In order to teach students "to explain the biology of sexual development and . . . sexual phenotype," Professor Bauer of Highpoint University developed a case study based on Caster Semenya, a South African Olympic athlete whose victory in the Berlin world championship in 2009 was challenged on the basis of her androgynous appearance. Professor Bauer scaffolded assignments, first asking students to read about the biology of sex and then having them construct, in small groups, a flowchart of "determinants of sexual phenotypes." After three more structured assignments, students applied their knowledge in a class debate about gender-neutral housing (Bauer, 2018).

If you can design your own assignments, what might you ask students to do that more closely mirrors the actual work of your discipline? Consider what resources you might need in order to feel more comfortable assigning something less traditional. Appendix 3 lists many disciplinary resources that offer examples of successful authentic assignments in your field.

Responding like a Coach, Not a Judge

Right now you might be wondering, but how do I grade these kinds of nontraditional assignments? It helps to think of responding to student work as a form of communicating, rather than a form of evaluating. This applies to nontraditional and traditional assignments alike. Giving students feedback can enable them to see what they're doing well, help them change course when necessary, and provide them with the knowledge and confidence to succeed in future courses. Appraising students' work also gives us useful feedback about our teaching. For example, if every student fails a quiz, you will probably ask yourself if your presentation of the material was unclear or if the quiz was poorly designed. If most of your final papers are disappointing, you might consider reworking the assignment the next time you teach the course, perhaps helping students build the skills needed to write a stronger paper.

All these strategies rest on one assumption: the primary purpose of grading is to help students learn, and not to sort or rank them. We believe that an effective teacher isn't necessarily someone who only gives a certain percentage of As, Bs Cs, Ds, or Fs, or who assigns difficult work, or who is inflexible. It's possible, for example, that in a skilled teacher's course most of the students achieve As because the teacher successfully helped them master the material. In contrast, assigning difficult work does little good if most of your students do not end up understanding it. Good teaching should be measured by *how far our students progress*, and this can be both cognitive (the skills and understanding they've gained) and affective (their increased sense of confidence and belonging).

Making Your Expectations Clear

Have you ever worked on an assignment for a professor and wondered if you were on the right track or felt demoralized when you got the assignment back and realized that you hadn't understood the directions? Without clear instructions students can feel that the course is a guessing game and that grades are determined by instructors' whims. An important aspect of helping students to learn is making your expectations clear. It is not coddling or dumbing down your course to explain what you want to see in students' work and how you are going to evaluate it. In addition to clear instructions for each summative or heavily weighted assignment, develop a *rubric*, or an explanation of how the assignment will be evaluated. Rubrics don't have to be complicated: it's more important that you use something that makes sense to you and helps you articulate how you plan to evaluate student work than using a particular format. You'll want to share the rubric with students *before* they begin their assignment and, if possible, discuss the rubric with them to address their questions and help them understand how you plan to use the rubric. This means avoiding vague language ("excellent writing") or relying too much on disciplinary jargon. There are two basic types of rubrics: holistic and analytic. *Holistic rubrics* give descriptions of each level of proficiency. Table 5 is an example (with prompt included) from one of Stephanie's sophomore level writing classes

The advantage of the holistic rubric is that it doesn't take a long time to create and it gives students a sense of what comprises each category. *Analytic rubrics* take longer to develop but they give more detailed feedback to students. An analytic rubric explains each level of a category within the

Table 5 Holistic Rubric

Conference-Style Essay Prompt: *Based on our discussion of what it means/is to be literate in the United States today, explore the answer to a research question in an academic, conference-style essay. Using the four to six sources from your annotated bibliography (as well as any other sources you see necessary), create and support a clear thesis that somehow answers our broad question of "What does it mean to be literate in the United States today?" Use your knowledge of argumentation to use sources in varied ways (e.g., background, exhibit, argument, method) to create a provocative and interesting argument.*

Length: 8–10 pages

Format: MLA or APA

Letter Grade	Points Earned	Criterion and Instructor Comments
A		An "A" paper lays out an interesting research question and clearly answers that question with its thesis. The thesis is well supported throughout the essay and source materials are incorporated to prove, extend, and/or nuance the writer's argument. Paragraphs have topic sentences and the writing is stylistically smooth. There are few to no surface errors and MLA or APA style is used correctly.
B		A "B" paper lays out an interesting research question and clearly answers that question with its thesis. The thesis is generally well supported throughout the essay but source material is not incorporated in the most effective ways. Paragraphs generally have topic sentences. There are few to no surface errors and MLA or APA style is used correctly.
C		A "C" paper lays out a research question but does not provide a clear thesis. The thesis is not generally well supported, and the structure of the essay is muddled and confusing. Surface errors significantly detract from a reader's ability to understand the author's argument.
D–F		A "D" or "F" paper does not provide a thesis. The essay is unclear and without purpose. Surface errors significantly detract from a reader's ability to understand the author's argument.

Table 6 Analytic Rubric

	Above Average (4)	Sufficient (3)	Developing (2)	Needs Improvement (1)
Clarity: Thesis supported by relevant information and ideas.	The central purpose of the student's work is clear and supporting ideas are always well focused. Details are relevant and enrich the work.	The central purpose of the student's work is clear and ideas are almost always focused in a way that supports the thesis. Relevant details illustrate the author's ideas.	The central purpose of the student's work is identified. Ideas are generally focused in a way that supports the thesis.	The purpose of the student's work is not well defined. Central ideas are not focused to support the thesis. Thoughts appear disconnected.
Organization: Sequencing of elements/ideas.	Information and ideas are presented in a logical sequence that flows logically and is engaging to the audience.	Information and ideas are presented in a logical sequence that is followed by the reader with little or no difficulty.	Information and ideas are presented in an order that the audience can follow with minimum difficulty.	Information and ideas are poorly sequenced (the author jumps around). The audience has difficulty following the thread of thought.
Mechanics: Correctness of grammar and spelling.	The mechanics of the document are accurate, and don't cause any interruption in the audience's understanding.	The readability of the work is minimally interrupted by errors.	Errors distract from the audience's ability to understand the work.	The readability of the work is seriously hampered by errors.

assignment. Table 6 is an example rubric for an academic essay adapted from DePaul University's Teaching Commons (Types of Rubrics, n.d.).

There are many rubric templates and examples of good rubrics. There is no one correct rubric—it really depends on what you're looking for in an assignment and what your students struggle with. The first couple of rubrics you create will probably take a bit of time and you may well end up revising them. That's typical. As you gain more experience with creating and grading assignments, rubrics will become easier to create. When you receive student work that does a good job of showing you the student has learned the skills and understandings you were hoping, take note! What specific evidence or demonstrations of learning are there? Can these help you to clarify and improve your rubric? The important thing is that you attempt to make it clear to students what you expect: this does not make the assignment easier, it makes it clearer and helps level the playing field for all students. If you're feeling ambitious, let students help you create the rubric for an assignment. Students perform better on tasks that they have some control over, and asking them to help create the rubric ensures that they better understand the assignment and creates more buy in.

When responding to student work, we strongly recommend that you hand back drafts as soon as you humanly (and humanely) can: this is for your students' benefit and your own sanity. Students need prompt feedback on their work so that they can correct errors and move forward. It's also helpful for students to receive your comments and assessments while their ideas are still fresh in their minds.

Responding to Students' Written Work

Responding to written work can be one of the most time-consuming parts of grading, but writing is one of the clearest ways students can demonstrate their understanding of a subject in their own voices. How can you respond to your students' written work in a way that helps them get better, rather than using your comments to justify the grade? Here is a distillation of what has been found to work best when responding to students' written work:

- Give students multiple opportunities to practice with low-stakes writing that isn't graded but receives credit for completion.
- Allow students to turn in drafts or proposals of their papers. Or, if you are willing to spend the time, schedule office hours where students can talk to you about their ideas before they write their first drafts.
- Focus on students' ideas and logic—not the mechanics of spelling, punctuation, or formatting—and give them suggestions on how to deepen or sharpen their ideas (Bean, 2011).
- Let students know about resources, such as the campus writing center, or online tools like the Purdue OWL or Grammarly. Don't spend your time correcting every error in your students' writing. You might also want to prepare a blanket statement that helps students know why you are directing them to those resources and what you hope they will gain from them. Your institution might also have additional resources for second language learners.
- When commenting on student papers, less is more! Give them targeted suggestions. If you have a hard time getting through their papers, decide how many minutes you can spend on each paper and set a timer.
- Consider having students submit the rubric for the assignment with their final papers and ask them to self-assess the strengths and weaknesses of their work according to the rubric before turning it in.
- Pick a couple of assignments and give students opportunities to revise these for a higher grade.

One noteworthy study looks at the effect of a specific way to frame comments on students' papers. The researchers found that when instructors communicated that they have high standards but that they are sure the students can meet those standards, this engendered trust and motivated students to take the opportunity to revise their essays, thereby improving their quality (Yaeger et al., 2014). This way of framing comments on student papers is called *wise feedback*.

Alternatives to Traditional Grading

There is a growing body of research that suggests that grades can decrease students' intrinsic motivation, their interest in a topic, and their creativity (Butler, 1988; Kohn, 2013; Blum, 2020). Based on this research and on some faculty's own unease about grading, a growing number of faculty have stopped using traditional forms of grading student work (Supiano, 2019). Instead of grading individual assignments, these faculty make extensive comments on their students' work, allow students to revise their assignments, encourage students to reflect on their own learning, and some even allow students to determine their final grades. Some colleges don't give students final grades, for example, New College of Florida, Evergreen State College, Hampshire College, Alverno, and others. New College of Florida explains their approach on their website in a statement, "Beyond Grading":

> We believe that detailed feedback on your individual strengths and weaknesses—as well as suggestions for improvement and further study—are much more valuable than a mere letter grade. . . . [N]arrative evaluations promote a noncompetitive learning environment with no fretting about your GPA and how you rank against your peers. Instead, you focus on the

> ways you can improve and develop the knowledge, experience, and critical and analytic thinking skills needed in the real world. (New College of Florida, n.d.)

What about the great majority of us who will teach at colleges where we are required to give final grades? You can still experiment with ways of de-emphasizing grading and increase the amount of formative (low-stakes or ungraded) feedback you give. For example, you might decide to use a "specifications" grading system, in which students decide which grade they're aiming for and then complete the assignments needed for each grade (Nilson, 2016). In this system, individual assignments are not given grades, but instead are marked "pass/fail" and given extensive comments. In order for this to work, instructors must give detailed "specifications" for each assignment so that students know what they need to produce in order to successfully get credit for the assignment.

As an example, Aeron and Stephanie successfully used this type of grading in a sophomore level literature course. Table 7 shows how we presented it to our students.

In order to count, all assignments needed to be completed "satisfactorily," which we made clear in the assignment rubrics. When Aeron used this type of grading in a senior undergraduate course on Victorian literature, she told the students that each assignment must be completed according to what she felt appropriate for an upper-level English course. In order to make this standard clear and help them meet it, Aeron assigned several short "close reading" papers early in the semester and gave students opportunities to revise and resubmit (with extensive feedback) until they had mastered the standard. Students were happy to have this chance to practice their skills and those who weren't

Table 7 Example Grading Specifications

We have designed a grading specification or schema so that you can tailor your work in this course to *suit your own goals*. We hope this will allow you to take more risks, experiment by going out of your comfort zone, and ultimately learn more deeply.

Column A: Foundational Assignments	Column B: Options
In-class reading quizzes*	Close-reading paper w/ sources (5 pp.)
3 short close reading papers for each major era (1-2 pp., 3 total)	*Humument* Project
10 weekly wiki posts (5 before spring break and 5 after)	Film adaptation analysis
Literary style identification quiz	Historical context Wiki
	Leading class discussion
	Innovation project: requires proposal

Notes. Class reading quizzes cannot be made up; however, the lowest two quizzes will be dropped.
For a C in the course: Complete all "foundational" assignments in Column A.
For a B: Complete all "foundational" assignments in Column A *and* **3** options from Column B.
For an A: Complete all "foundational" assignments in Column A *and* **4** options from Column B.

as invested in the course seemed content with their lower grades. This approach front-loads your work but results in much better papers later in the semester.

When Aeron asked students to reflect (anonymously) on the impact of this nontraditional form of grading, many of them remarked that it gave them space to be more innovative and take more risks in their literary analysis and in their writing. In a new student experience course that Stephanie taught, she also used this kind of specifications grading system to give students from a variety of backgrounds a lot of choice in how they approached the course. These freshmen were surprised by so much choice, but similarly commented that they liked having the options to choose which assignments to focus on to make the most out of the course. In a graduate course on pedagogy that Aeron taught, there were students from many disciplines with varied levels of teaching experience. The goal of the class was for each student to develop their own informed pedagogical practice. It would have been difficult to grade them according to one standard or, even worse, grade them against each other. They had a lot of intrinsic motivation to write good teaching statements and to practice their teaching skills, since they knew that these would help them on the job market.

Are Grades Important?

No matter what assignments you design, or even if you adopt alternative grading schemes, grading can be fraught because most of us are invested in the idea that grades are meaningful. When Aeron first started teaching as a beginning graduate student she agonized over her students' final grades: for example, should she really give one of her strongest students a B+ instead of an A, because he'd missed four classes and she had a strict attendance policy? As someone who had been a high-achieving undergraduate herself, and who was in a graduate program where earning one B meant forfeiting summer funding, grades held a lot of personal meaning and tangible value. As TAs you are in the position of having to judge a student's work and in some cases, a student's honesty: Did a student really write a paper that seems significantly better than all their previous work? Did a student miss the exam for a valid reason, or did they just skip? Sometimes students' final grades don't mirror the effort and contributions we see in class; conversely, some students may seem disengaged or be regularly absent and still ace all their graded work. The students Aeron taught while she was in graduate school, at a competitive flagship state university, were high achievers and often would argue about their grades. Every time Aeron gave certain students grades lower than an A, she anticipated pushback; she wonders now if that pressure biased her grading in unconscious ways. When students challenge our grading, it can feel like (and sometimes is) a way of challenging our authority in the classroom.

For all the power we imbue grades with, they are often not accurate, objective, or motivational tools for learning. Many of our grading practices come from how we were taught, which in turn come from how our teachers were taught, and so on. Sadly, these grading traditions are rarely based on any empirical evidence that they are the most effective in promoting learning. The history of grades in American higher education shows that there never has been a perfectly objective way to measure a student's ability or intelligence. Grades were developed in the 19th century during industrialization with the increased interest in standardization, and our entire letter grade system wasn't widely used in colleges until the 1940s. Grades were not developed to help students learn, but to create standards that could be recognized between schools. Grading on a curve, for example, was a response to research in the early 20th century that seemed to show that there was a natural curve to the level of intellectual ability in the general population. However, the fairness of grading on a curve has been widely discredited (Humphreys, Johnson, & Johnson 1982; Dubey, 2010).

There is an entire body of literature dedicated to the history of grades in American education, and much of that research shows that traditional methods of grading don't motivate students to learn, nor do they provide reliable information about how much they've learned (Schinske

& Tanner, 2014; Davidson, 2017). Even as early as 1930, research revealed that a single paper received markedly different grades from different instructors—and even from the same instructor at different times (Eells, 1930). In his recent book, *Grading for Equity*, Joe Feldman describes how grading practices in K-12 also vary widely and can result in inequitable treatment of students. He cites examples where students who show the same understanding of content received different final grades because of the idiosyncrasies in individual teachers' grading systems, such as points off for late work, heavily weighted subjective categories ("participation," "effort," or "citizenship"), or even because a student's assignment was turned in with ripped paper. As a result, final grades did not reflect students' mastery of the material; instead, it reflected their ability to follow (sometimes arbitrary) instructions. These variations in teachers' grading systems also have the effect of sending students confusing messages about their abilities and encouraging students to treat grades as an arbitrary system that can be gamed. Some grading practices also penalize students who begin our courses less prepared, even when they eventually master the material by the end of the semester. For example, if the first paper or quiz is weighted heavily then students who initially struggle in the course but who achieve excellent work at the end will be unable to achieve a high grade.

Unfortunately, high failure rates are sometimes seen as reflecting high standards. Some introductory courses are treated by departments and programs as "weed out" courses with expected high rates of failure. Think about what that means—we ask students to sign up and pay for courses with the presumption that a large portion of them cannot be successful. Craig Nelson, emeritus professor of biology at Indiana University, describes how he challenged his own initial misconceptions about teaching and grading in his now-famous essay, "Dysfunctional Illusions of Rigor" (Nelson, 2010). When he began teaching, Nelson believed in the following common assumptions about teaching:

- Hard courses weed out weak students.
- Traditional methods of instruction are unbiased and equally fair to a range of diverse students of good ability.
- If we cover more content, the students will learn more content. (Nelson 2010)

However, after examining relevant research on active learning, Nelson concluded that, "when students fail, it is often due to inappropriate pedagogy" and not just students' lack of effort or preparedness (2010, p. 180). Research shows that being more thoughtful and intentional about how we design, teach, and grade may foster greater student success without sacrificing high standards.

The history of grades may make grading schemes like "un-grading" or specifications grading not seem so radical after all. And, while these strategies may seem out of bounds for you as a graduate instructor, they are also an extension of how we've tried to frame assignments and feedback throughout this chapter: our job as instructors is to foster student learning, not to divide students into categories. For this reason, we urge you to use assignments as tools to give students feedback on their learning. Skeptics could argue that strategies like un-grading allow students to produce B work but end up with an A in the course. One could also argue that more creative or authentic assignments take up valuable course time and limit the amount of content that can be covered. This is true. But the more important questions, to us, are do the students learn more, are they more engaged in the course, do they put in more effort and take more ownership in their work? By de-emphasizing grades as a ranking measure or a method of gatekeeping in your discipline and creating assignments that allow students to perform their understanding, you'll be better situated to focus on your students' learning and perhaps even begin to change expectations about who can be successful in your field.

KEY TAKEAWAYS

- Make it clear how assignments are linked to the course learning outcomes.
- Break larger assignments down into small, more manageable parts.
- Consider incorporating more low-stakes, formative assignments to give students the opportunity to practice their skills and understanding.
- Students learn best when they receive prompt and clear feedback on their work.

CHAPTER 7

WHAT ARE OTHER GRADUATE STUDENTS EXPERIENCING?

In Stephanie's first year of graduate school, she and her office mate were teaching the same courses so they decided to design all their teaching materials collaboratively. Not only did this help with their teaching workloads, it gave them a built-in sounding board for reflecting after each unit. It was a small decision, but it set Stephanie up to think of her teaching as a topic for reflection and supportive collaboration. Graduate students face many common teaching hurdles, but rarely get an opportunity to share experiences and learn from one another's setbacks. This is likely because academia values unique contributions and individual success. At its worst, these values come at the detriment of good teaching—which is strengthened by critical reflection on what went wrong, a willingness to take risks and be vulnerable, and productive collaboration among colleagues. We hope that you are in a graduate program that cultivates and supports you in developing collaborative teaching. However, if you aren't, this chapter provides you with reflections from other graduate student teachers and gives you a blueprint for the kinds of conversations you might want to initiate with your peers.

We've interviewed several current graduate teaching assistants, instructors, and professors at different stages in their careers to chat about what was or would have been helpful to them as they began teaching in graduate school. We started by asking each of them what preparation they received for teaching, what major challenges they faced, and what they've learned as a result. Despite their differences in disciplines and preparation, they all faced challenges throughout their teaching careers—when they were beginners and any time they had to tackle new curriculum, modalities, or even just a new student population. We encourage you to frame challenges in teaching as pedagogical puzzles to be solved, rather than the personal shortcomings of you or your students. At the beginning of your teaching career you may feel like you are pretending at disciplinary expertise when you yourself are being taught by senior faculty with CVs full of publications and presentations. You may be teaching a course you placed out of as an undergraduate or teaching an introductory course that spans material outside of your area of focus. Are you already starting to feel the creep of imposter syndrome, that feeling that you have fooled people into believing that you are capable of teaching? Almost everyone feels like this at one time or another. It helps to avoid false comparisons between your own beginning attempts and more seasoned graduate students' and faculty's seemingly polished teaching. We all start at the beginning.

Teaching What You Don't Know

While a graduate student in anthropology, David cobbled together funding by teaching in several different departments. He was a TA for a large lecture course in anthropology, and he also taught biology labs, graded for an online psychology course, and taught a one-credit course for graduate students on pedagogy. For the anthropology course, he was expected to learn by watching how the professor lectured and to grade student work based on his best "gut" estimate of what an A, B, or C paper was. For the psychology course, he was encouraged to read along with the content the students were studying and grade their online discussion posts based on word count and completion; he was discouraged from any additional participation. These weren't satisfying experiences for David.

Luckily, he also had experiences where he could try his hand at designing the learning for his students. In the anthropology course, his professor was away for a week at a conference. She left instructions that he should provide a lecture on kinship models. With little more than a barebones outline, David had a lot of room to flesh out what the class would look like. He chose a learning activity he had found exciting as an undergrad to help students apply kinship models to their own lives. He explained, "When I was a student, I liked having something to do, time for processing, and attaching more information to [the concept we are learning]. It's like the process I use as an anthropologist where we collect the data, analyze and think about it, and then see what kinds of information we can attach to it."

David brought this same anthropological approach to teaching a one-credit course on pedagogy. After speaking with the director of the Center for Teaching and Learning who oversaw the course and the dean of graduate studies about the mission and purpose of the course, he realized that the class had multiple purposes: (1) To help graduate students understand basic concepts in adult learning theory, course design, and the science of teaching and learning; and (2) for him to model effective teaching. His teaching grew a lot, in part because he got to teach the course for five semesters, but also because he had to do a lot of research to make the course useful for the students. David felt like he was most successful when he used examples and activities that were aligned to his students' disciplines. "My brain works like an anthropologist, a professional learner, and people responded really well to examples that allowed them to personally connect with the material."

In teaching biology labs, David found that this "professional learner" approach also worked well. David wasn't a biologist, and he didn't pretend to be for his students. Instead, when a student asked a question he didn't know, he would tell them "I don't know, but let's figure it out together." When we asked David if students were frustrated by his lack of experience in the discipline, he said "No. I think they just figured it was part of the learning." Students seemed to appreciate that he was willing to help them figure out tough problems, and it also gave some students the chance to be experts in the lab as well. The training to teach these classes was really limited but the process of doing it was illuminating for David as he developed his own teaching style.

Like David, many of you might be asked to teach outside your area of specialization, even, in some cases, outside your home departments. Although this can be daunting, it can also prepare you for most full-time academic jobs in which we are required to be generalists. Therese Huston, in her book *Teaching What You Don't Know,* offers practical strategies for teaching outside of your area of expertise:

- Establish your credibility through conscientious teaching: be approachable, communicate often, make your expectations clear, and show your students that you are committed to their success.
- Be genuine and never pretend to have more expertise than you have. It's okay to admit when you do not know the answer. (As David relates, you can find out in collaboration with students.)
- Embrace being a beginner. Although in an ideal situation we would only be teaching our narrow area of specialization, Huston cites research that shows novices are often better teachers. Specifically, nonexperts are often better at putting concepts into everyday language and anticipating typical mistakes. (Huston, 2009)

You can also take a look at Appendix 1 for a condensed checklist to help you create a course on a short timeline.

Navigating the Hidden Curriculum

Watching her graduate professors, Beatrice felt like she was learning both how to be a college educator and how not to be a college educator. Her department, sports administration, was largely hands-off during the first four years of her program. At the end of her fourth year, her entire cohort was surprised to hear that they should have already completed their comprehensive exams and should have been planning pieces of their proposals throughout their coursework. COVID-19 was changing the budget landscape for her institution, and it seemed like their cohort was being rushed out as a result.

Beatrice was also embarrassed; this seemed another example of the hidden curriculum, or secret set of rules and expectations within graduate school. She was reminded many times of her status as one of the few Black students in the program. For example, during her coursework, a professor criticized her for not speaking enough in class even though the syllabus did not explicitly state any expectations for classroom participation. He then compared her to the two other African American students who were more outspoken and questioned whether she was a good fit for her program. Beatrice mustered up her courage and asked him why he was only comparing her to those two students when there were several quiet students in the course. She asked the professor if he was concerned about the quality of the work she had submitted for the course, and he admitted that he wasn't. Why then was he concerned about her "fit" for the program, she asked? The professor dropped the issue, but the conversation shook her confidence. Did he really think she didn't belong in the program? She had been told when she was younger that she talked too much in class, so she was self-conscious about being perceived as dominating the conversation. She was trying hard to make all the right decisions. Beatrice suffered another blow to her confidence when she was asked to rewrite one of her comprehensive exams. When she and her advisor questioned the professor asking for the rewrite, he said that her answer was correct, but he just wanted her to write it differently. When her advisor pushed for further clarification, it seemed that the professor simply wanted Beatrice to write a longer answer but had given her no indication of this in the question prompt.

These experiences made Beatrice feel like an outsider in

higher education, but they weren't new to her. She had grown up in a mostly white, middle-class suburb and was always aware of her "difference" as a young Black woman. At college, however, while attending an HBCU (Historically Black College or University) she felt a different sense of isolation. She was too light skinned, she didn't talk the right way, and she didn't like the right foods. She got involved in sports and used her athleticism to help her grow her sense of belonging. As part of the team, she didn't feel like she had to pretend to be someone other than herself. In sports everyone spoke directly and helped one another for the benefit of the team. Her experience as an athlete significantly shaped who she wanted to be as a graduate student and as a teacher. She didn't want to be someone who used a mouthful of jargon to describe an idea she could explain simply, and she didn't want to be someone who had to butter up people in charge to get them to advocate for her. She wanted her hard work to speak for itself and she had imagined graduate school as a place where she could learn deeply in her coursework; gain research, teaching, and professional experience; and move on. She didn't want graduate school to define her entire sense of self.

With completion looming sooner than she had planned, she decided to advocate for the opportunity to teach an introduction to sports administration course, rather than the fitness courses she had been teaching for the last four years. No one in her cohort even knew if it was possible to get to teach this course, but Beatrice once again gathered the courage to ask for what she needed. Her early teaching experiences, mostly classes like Pilates and yoga, did not give her a lot of experience teaching in her field, as the preparation for those courses was entirely focused on how to take roll and ensure students completed a health waiver.

Without any preparation, Beatrice had been on her own to navigate these early teaching experiences and she found that her honesty was often mistaken for incompetence. Initially, she was frank with students about not knowing something about a particular exercise or posture. She would tell them that she needed to research their question and then get back to them. This resulted in negative comments on the end of semester evaluations in which students claimed that she didn't know what she was doing. It's true, Beatrice wasn't an expert in these areas, but her department also hadn't offered any training or preparation to teach these courses. The supervisor of the program advised her not to admit when she didn't know the answer to a question.

As she prepared to teach her introduction to sports management course, she tried to learn from her mistakes in more strategic ways. Instead of ignoring questions she didn't know, she planned to use student questions to nudge them to enhance their own learning by seeking out additional resources. While she was nervous to be teaching this course for the first time online, she also felt thankful that in an online course she would have time to research and respond to student questions instead of being put on the spot. She received helpful advice from a new assistant professor who recently joined her department. He was forthright with her about similar challenges that he had experienced when he began teaching and walked her through the approaches he had adopted. Beatrice wished more professors in her department shared this kind of information and offered more realistic advice for how to navigate graduate school and teaching.

Beatrice's experience speaks to the challenges of being a "first," an "only," or just being part of a group that is underrepresented in higher education. Despite her very best efforts, and even with the advocacy of people like her advisor, she was often blindsided by expectations that seemed brand new or only applied to her. This can shake the confidence of even the most capable graduate student. It can also be difficult to discuss openly, because most of us do not want to dwell on embarrassing moments. In graduate school, where competence and knowledge are highly valued, it can feel deeply shameful to find out you don't know something or haven't followed the right steps for success. If you've experienced this, we want you to know that you aren't alone in that feeling. Even if no one else in your department or cohort is admitting to it, people are stumbling every day.

To greater and lesser extents, academic departments are not structured or prepared to help you with these feelings of shame. Few departments are having realistic conversations with graduate students about the job market, and even fewer know how to address graduate students' mental health and well-being challenges. Like Beatrice, you too might encounter scholars in your field who will question how you are doing graduate school without any justification. What they don't want to say, and maybe can't even admit to themselves, is that you aren't doing things the way that they did them. As we've mentioned earlier, anyone can fall prey to imposter syndrome, but some people are more likely to be made to feel like imposters within their own department.

Let's be clear, Beatrice faces far greater scrutiny than white male instructors face when they admit gaps in their knowledge. While David's biology students appreciated his frankness about not knowing all the answers, Beatrice's students saw her honesty as ground for complaint. Graduate students face pressure to receive high student evaluations of their teaching and to avoid negative comments that may draw the attention of their department. However, numerous studies show that student evaluations of teaching contain gender and racial biases (Holman, Key, & Kreitzer, 2019). Beatrice, like other women of color in the academy, commonly found that students question her professional competence more than they do that of white male instructors (Vargas, 2002; Nettles 2002; Tuitt et al., 2011). There is a growing body of research that shows that students' evaluations of teaching contain biases against women, faculty of color, and instructors who speak English as a second language (Drake, 2019; Subtirelu, 2015). The American Sociological Association has issued a statement that cites this research and calls for departments to stop using teaching evaluations as the primary measure of teaching effectiveness (2019). If you find yourself, like Beatrice, struggling to navigate hidden standards or changing expectations consider the following:

- Ask one of your mentors to observe you teach and use this observation as documentation of your teaching effectiveness, as a supplement to or in replacement of student evaluations of teaching.
- Use Sindhumathi Revuluri's (2018) many mentors model and seek out individuals who can help you check your impressions. If this isn't available in your department, look to your campus support centers (La Raza, African American Student Center, Asian and Pacific Islander Student Center, or LGBTQIA+ Center) to see if they have a list of faculty advisors who might be able to offer an outside perspective.
- See Chapter 3 for strategies in creating stronger classroom communities and inviting students to co-construct class knowledge.
- See Chapter 6 on creating assignments that help students develop greater ownership of their learning.

Teaching as an International Student and Negotiating Cultural Differences

Ahmed came to the United States from Egypt as a Fulbright Scholar. Although he had experience teaching in Egypt, he was very nervous about teaching in the United States. As a Fulbright Scholar, he received a week of training, but it didn't cover all the cultural and pedagogical differences between his country and the United States. For example, typically in Egypt there is no syllabus, no lesson plan, and not much interaction between the professor and the students: the professor lectures and the students listen respectfully and don't argue. When Ahmed began teaching in the US, he was nervous that the students wouldn't understand his English and that they wouldn't accept differences in his mannerisms or his appearance. Even anticipating these cultural differences, what happened on the first day completely surprised him: while Ahmed was lecturing, a student put his feet up on a chair. This would be considered incredibly disrespectful in Egypt, and Ahmed was shocked and worried that this student's behavior indicated an extreme lack of respect.

However, instead of angrily confronting the student, Ahmed sought advice from a professor in his department who explained that the student's action was probably just a sign of the informal American classroom, and not a direct affront to him. He also introduced Ahmed to another graduate student from Egypt who had lots of teaching experience, and this graduate student became his mentor. Ahmed went on to win a university-wide teaching award and teach a course for other international graduate teaching assistants. In this class, he talked openly about cultural differences in the American college classroom and provided a supportive space where international teaching assistants could troubleshoot difficulties or frustrating situations that occurred in their classrooms. One of the common worries that international graduate students had is that their accents would make it difficult for students to understand them. For good reason, as undergraduates often do complain in course evaluations that they cannot understand nonnative speakers of English. Ahmed told his fellow international graduate students,

> Do not be ashamed of your accents. Your accent is a sign that you are so intelligent and valued that you've been brought all the way here to another country to study. There is a difference between having an accent and not being understood. Address the issue early on with your students. Tell them where you are from and reassure them that they will get used to your accent over time. In the meanwhile, speak as clearly as you can and write down key words and phrases on the board.

Ahmed's experience illustrates how useful it can be to see yourself in context and identify a few sage advisors (either senior TAs or faculty whose teaching you admire) to help you check your perceptions of incidents in the classroom (Revuluri, 2018). Understandably, though, it can be hard to remember this when you are far from home and so many things are unfamiliar. While universities are excited to attract the more than 370,000 international graduate students studying in the US (Institute of International Education, 2020), there are even fewer resources geared toward supporting them as teachers. You might experience a situation like Ahmed's as an international student or perhaps you are simply teaching in a different region or cultural environment from where you grew up. As a student in Pennsylvania, Stephanie regularly addressed her teachers' questions with a short "yes" or "no" without any trouble but received a swift rebuke for not addressing teachers with the expected "yes ma'am" or "no sir" once she moved to Tennessee. Politeness and respect map differently across cultures and even communities, so don't take for granted that you and your students are working with the same set of expectations.

In general, as Ahmed learned quickly, US classrooms do tend toward a more casual atmosphere. The use of first names, vernacular language or slang, casual dress or posture are all common. "Although there are many differences in social, economic, and educational levels in the US, there is a theme of equality that runs through social relationships," Stacy Kizer points out in Vanderbilt University's *International Teaching Assistant's Guide*. This casual atmosphere might also extend to the kinds of questions students ask you about yourself. Depending on your comfort level, you can even use this to your advantage. Aparna Hebbani (Hebbani and Hendrix, 2014) developed rapport with her students by sharing her experiences as a new mom and her observations on American football (p. 68). Students might also be curious about where you are from, how much time you've spent in the United States, or what other languages you know. Although she had openly talked about being from Taiwan and the process of obtaining permanent residency in the US, Yea-Wen Chen was still unsure how she felt when a student asked her if she was an immigrant during her intercultural communications class (2014). Start thinking about how much you want to disclose to students, and how you plan to respond to their curiosity. Remember, you're under no obligation to disclose anything that makes you feel uncomfortable or entertain racist or hostile remarks. If you aren't sure if a question is simply curious or offensive, pay attention to how your other students react. If the class shows concern or seems nervous about your response, the question might have crossed a line. But if no one seems to react, or if they seem earnestly interested, then the question is likely just a way for your students to get to know you better. Like Ahmed, however, you can always check your assumptions with your colleagues if you aren't sure. Also, see chapter 5 on navigating challenges in the classroom to better understand the circumstances of many college students in the US and to learn about the differences between rude, disruptive, and hostile behavior.

Creating a Teaching Community

Callie was in a master's program for literature at a minority-serving research university. Like many humanities graduate students, she taught composition courses. Unlike many of the graduate students we interviewed, Callie took a two-week teaching practicum and she was given one fully prepared unit to get through the first month of the semester. The practicum also required graduate student teachers to work in small groups to design their second sequence together.

Despite this preparation, the first day of class was rough. As a young instructor, not much older than her students, she really didn't feel like she had a lot of authority in the classroom and she had an anxiety attack after class. Luckily, her fellow instructors from the teaching practicum decided to continue to work together and co-construct their sections for the rest of the semester. This small group of instructors met weekly to develop assignments and lessons and to reflect on how things were going in the classroom. They also voluntarily observed one another's teaching, which helped Callie get a sense of different teaching styles. Callie found the weekly meetings incredibly helpful as she tried to figure out how to handle the different (and often unfamiliar to her) ways that students needed her to accommodate their learning. Although Callie was teaching in the same institution where she had earned her BA, she was surprised by the complex challenges her students brought to her classes. As an undergraduate, she had done well in a traditional learning environment, but she soon realized that her students often faced very different challenges from those she experienced as an undergrad. What should she do to support a student who seemed to be disrupting other learners? How should she respond to a student who needed accommodations due to a chronic health issue? What should she do to meet the needs of a request from the accessibility services?

Callie had been given the advice to "model your teaching from someone who inspires you," but she found that this didn't work for her at all. Some of her own formative teachers had been demanding, and at times inflexible about deadlines. Although this strict approach was effective for her as an undergraduate, she began to wonder if these notions of rigor were the most useful for helping all her students succeed. She struggled for much of that first semester with trying to balance maintaining her sense of authority while crafting an authentic teaching persona. "You need to figure out who you are as a teacher," she advised. "Maybe allow yourself to be vulnerable and tell students when you make mistakes, and that you are new at this process too."

The weekly meetings she had with fellow graduate instructors encouraged her to figure out how to be more flexible as an instructor and how to structure her assignments so that all students had a chance to succeed. She learned a lot from her co-teachers about how to construct an assignment prompt and craft activities and readings that would help prepare students for the assignment. Each assignment, reading, and learning activity was vetted across six sections of the course. Callie and her co-teachers had many conversations assessing how their students performed on assignments, and they found ways to adjust their teaching to be more effective. This practice of refining her teaching in a supportive environment gave Callie a lot of confidence in making her own decisions as an instructor, and in developing her own style and persona. It also allowed her to take a step back and observe what was happening holistically in her class—a process that's now ingrained in her practice.

Callie's struggle navigating the expectations of her instructors and formulating her own expectations as an instructor is a common challenge. *Rigor* is a much used word in higher education that is often used to signify high standards and precision. However, as one definition explains it, rigor means "harsh inflexibility in opinion, temper, or judgment; the quality of being unyielding or inflexible; an act or instance of strictness, severity, or cruelty" (Merriam Webster's Collegiate Dictionary). How can this be the standard by which we measure teaching? We all want our students to work hard and meet high standards, but does this necessarily mean that we must be "harsh" and "inflexible" or "severe and cruel"? There is no research suggesting that this approach works; in fact, an inflexible approach generally rewards students lucky enough not to be facing hardships or who already believe they belong in college. We're asking you to do the much harder work of figuring out ways to give your students multiple on-ramps to success.

Callie's experience also demonstrates the usefulness of a teaching community in graduate school. This community might be other graduate student instructors in your program, at your institution, or even in online spaces like Twitter. It's an advantage if those folks have different approaches from your own or different teaching experiences—then you all have something to learn and share with one another. One strategy is to ask your graduate coordinator to give you a list of other graduate instructors and then reach out to them. If you're taking a teaching seminar, ask folks to meet informally outside of class. Plan for how you will work together and what your shared expectations will be. Consider these questions:

- How often will you meet and how—in person, virtually, or checking in over email?
- What work will you share and what should everyone prepare for each check-in?

By working closely with her co-teachers, Callie gained confidence and learned about different ways to address teaching challenges. She began to grow into her own teaching practice, one that was more aware of and responsive to student needs.

Taking a Biology Lab Online

As a graduate student, Swati taught in a large and well-run biology program at a competitive university where she took a semester-long seminar on teaching biology. The professor leading the seminar largely used his personal teaching experiences to guide the coursework and gave the TAs several opportunities to try different strategies out with one another. As a graduate student, she was very comfortable in the classroom and felt prepared to teach both the biology lecture and lab. Then, in her first job as a part-time instructor at another large state university she was offered the chance to teach her course and lab online to increase her teaching load. (There was also some special funding attached to teaching online, which incentivized both the faculty and the department to create more online courses.) Swati had never taught online before, but she was eager to do more for the department and hopefully land a full-time teaching position, so she volunteered to develop online versions of the course and the lab.

In graduate school, Swati had relied on the example of the professor teaching her practicum, her own college experiences, and those of her fellow graduate students. This was helpful, but it did not give her any guidance how to move an F2F course online. She dove into the literature of online learning, starting with *Conquering the Content* (Smith 2008), and found that much of her teaching translated well to the online environment. The classroom lectures, which she normally punctuated with iClicker questions, became 2–5-minute narrated PowerPoint videos that each culminated with a quiz. While she was encouraged by this initial success, creating an online lab was more challenging. There were several manuals and kits she could adopt, but none of them aligned well with what she did in F2F teaching and the kits were incredibly expensive. Her online lab was only one credit, so it needed to be manageable for students in terms of time and resources; she needed to think about what students had access to and what a student alone could be expected to manage. After doing her research, she created some labs that online students could do with items found in a grocery store. In other more complex labs, she demonstrated the experiment and then asked students to analyze and interpret the results. Her focus was on the concepts most important for students to learn and retain as they moved forward in their degree programs. She also allowed students to work in groups to help them share the burden of the process and to develop the strong collaborative skills scientists need in a lab environment.

Although her online students tended to ask more thoughtful questions about the course material (most likely because every student was required to contribute written questions), she also recognized that it was easier for her online students to misunderstand or misinterpret her communication because they couldn't hear her tone or see her nonverbal cues. Clear communication became increasingly important to her after moving her classes online, and this realization motivated her to work on greater clarity in her F2F courses. Swati mentored the TAs in her lab to write clearer quiz and exam questions—training she wished she received as a graduate student. She also looked for more ways to help students build greater collaborative skills online and considered, moving forward, requiring the labs to be group assignments. Although students have the option to work in groups, many of her online students attempted to do the assignments on their own. In Swati's words, "Group proximity and dynamics are challenging in all classes but can be even harder online. Science is cooperative and it's tough to build that skill organically online."

Have you ever thought, or heard someone say, "You can't teach *that* online!"? Swati's example illustrates both the triumphs and challenges of taking a course online that is highly interactive and largely dependent on group cooperation. Her experience also reflects a common occurrence where the newest, often most precarious, educators in a department are asked to take on the responsibility of developing online courses. This can be a great opportunity to have your work and talent recognized, and it can be incredibly daunting. Teaching online can also be a way to tap into additional funding sources. As a graduate student, Stephanie volunteered for opportunities to teach online and hybrid versions of her department's writing courses to garner additional funding. (This experience proved useful when she decided not to pursue a traditional tenure track and instead work in online faculty development.)

Like the scientist she is, Swati started her research into teaching online with a literature review. She knew there were resources for teaching online that she hadn't been exposed to in graduate school. How could she ensure that students would have the necessary learning experience in an online lab? Using her backward design principles and creativity helped her determine that certain labs could be done with grocery store supplies, while she could focus on the scientific process in labs that would have been too pricey and time consuming to ask students to do on their own.

Swati's design prowess has gotten her far, but there are two issues she's still grappling with: her online students are not collaborating as consistently and deeply as their F2F counterparts and they are not as capable at interpreting her tone in written communication. The latter is often referred to as *instructor presence* in an online course. When there is a strong instructor presence in an online class, students tend to have a better understanding of the intent of the instructor's communication, regardless of whether that communication happens in video, audio, or by text. Already, Swati has been allowing her online students to work in groups, but few take the opportunity. She's considering requiring them to work in groups for at least one lab to ensure they get some experience collaborating as scientists. She might prepare a poll or short survey at the beginning of the semester to help students identify times and days that they may be able to work with a group in a synchronous web conferencing session. This is a small change she can make to her online lab that would help her tackle the lack of student-to-student collaboration. In addition to observing the quality of the subsequent lab reports, Swati could also have students complete a short survey describing the differences in their experience of the group lab versus their individual labs. When you are approaching a pedagogical problem specific to your field it can be helpful to look to multidisciplinary books, like this one, and also seek out one of the several journals, websites, or conferences that addresses online teaching in your field, specifically. This can be a great place to learn about discipline-specific challenges like taking a biology lab online. If you get offered the chance to take a course online, be sure to see chapter 2 and try out the online course map.

Engaging Students in a General Education Course

In the final year of his PhD program at a large flagship state university, Edward was the instructor of record for a survey of early American history, a general education requirement. Although he had served as a discussion leader for several courses, this was the first course he taught himself. His experience of history was very content heavy and traditionally taught through lectures. Edward also lectured, and he prided himself on his ability to tell stories that engaged students in the material. For his first course, he chose to use *The American Yawp: A Massively Collaborative Open U.S. History Textbook*, which was free and available online. However, his lectures did not just cover the material that students read. Instead, he consulted two other textbooks and used class time to present other information and perspectives on history. This was also his strategy to encourage students to attend class.

Although there were a few students who sat in the front and answered questions, he was disappointed that many students seemed disengaged in the course: some seemed to show up to check off a box for their general education requirements. Edward wanted to change that. He believed that all students, no matter their majors, can gain valuable skills from studying history: that history gives us an understanding of our own positionality and shows us how to make judgements when confronted with incomplete information. Edward decided that instead of jumping right into course content the next time he taught the course, he would devote the first week of the semester to a conceptual understanding of the big questions and themes in American history. In order to engage them in these large questions, he asked students to write about what they thought were the most interesting and important issues in American history: "If you want them to be interested, you have to be interested in them," he pointed out.

Next, he designed an activity to help students learn how to read primary sources, a key disciplinary skill. He showed students three maps: the Waldsmuller map from 1507, a map showing overlapping indigenous nations, and a map of the southwest from the 1700s. The purpose of the map activity was to show them how maps illuminate certain types of information while obscuring others. Before he showed them the maps, he asked them to list the types of data that could be put in a map, then he wrote those on the board and discussed them. The class came up with the usual characteristics, such as terrain, elevation, political boundaries, water features, but also included things like demographics, weather, mythology, aspirations, and knowledge versus conjecture. He explained that mapmaking is a political act: "creating maps was a key part of the European efforts to conquer the Americas, and the very act of making a map gave them a sense of ownership and control over a large, vast space." Using a native lands map, he asked students to consider the political project of mapping over the US with indigenous nations. He used the final map, the Alzate map, to show them how limited European information and power could be, an exercise he learned from his undergraduate professor at Stanford, Dr. Richard White.

He chose this activity in order to get students talking early in the semester, even before they had content expertise. The activity also got them practicing some of the skills that they needed to use in the class, like discriminating between kinds of data, determining how accurate data might be, and learning how to approach visual sources with a critical eye. The activity also gave students a way to understand some themes of the course—how nations project power, how they represent their own authority over territory, and how indigenous people are full-fledged actors in American history.

Edward faced a common problem: teaching a large general education course that students are required to take and that they often view as an unnecessary requirement. Although he wasn't given any teaching training from his department, he was passionate about the study of history and wasn't satisfied engaging only a few students. This dissatisfaction was his strength because it inspired him to experiment. Edward intuitively believed that getting students to think about the big questions was worth sacrificing a few class sessions of content. Although Edward hadn't taken courses on college pedagogy, he deployed a key active learning strategy: asking students to do the work of thinking and analyzing instead of merely listening to the instructor's analysis. Perhaps Edward's background (both his mother and grandmother are teachers) accounts for his learner-centered approach.

Or, it might have been his own experiences in college where students were engaged, active participants in their courses.

Often, our best innovations and teaching practices come from our love for the subject and our frustration when the course does not seem to allow students to access the wonder and beauty of our field. Another move that Edward made was that he didn't default to the assumption that most of the students were incapable of becoming passionate about history. Edward's approach to redesigning his introductory history course mirrors a larger movement within the discipline of history: the "uncoverage model." Led by historians Sam Wineburg, Lendol Calder, David Voelker, and Joel Sipress, proponents of the uncoverage model argue that just because you cover the material, doesn't mean the students have learned it. Instead, they argue, we should construct introductory courses around methods of engaging students in our discipline's ways of knowing. In the case of history, this has been described as "participation in a contested academic discourse in which rival truth claims are subjected to rigorous scrutiny on the basis of evidence drawn from the human past" (Sipress & Voelker, 19).

If you have the kind of flexibility Edward did, be sure to see the sections in Chapter 6 on authentic assignments, un-grading, and alternatives to traditional grading.

Developing a Growth Mindset toward Your Students

Katherine cared about her teaching and, while in graduate school, had been a recipient of a university-wide teaching award. When she began her first job at a regional comprehensive university, teaching courses that she had taught as a graduate student (anatomy and physiology as well as biomechanics), her strategies didn't work as well. Her new students struggled in biomechanics courses, which relied upon foundational knowledge of anatomy, physics, and math. Students reacted negatively to teaching strategies she had been using for years as a graduate student. Her teaching mimicked what she had experienced as a student: mostly lectures, quizzes, and exams. She had been discouraged from spending too much time thinking about her teaching; graduate students who had done so were held up as examples of what not to do.

When she reached out to her department chair for guidance, she was told that "these students" weren't as good at math as those she had encountered in graduate school. This bothered her because her students were predominately students of color from the local area and she objected to the idea that they couldn't learn math. Her chair recommended that she make her course easier; however, Katherine decided not to lower her course standards. Instead, she decided to work harder to meet her students where they were and to spend more time understanding what their foundational knowledge was and how to build on it. "Student resistance let me know that something was different," Katherine recalled. "If you are doing the same thing over and over, but more students are failing, it's our responsibility to figure out what's going wrong." She took a hard look at her curriculum to determine what big ideas, essential knowledge, and skills students needed for further semesters or in professional fields relying on biomechanics. She gave a lot of thought to what it should mean to pass her class, met with faculty who taught courses that used hers as a prerequisite, and focused on modeling the essential knowledge and skills. She then created ways that students could practice and receive feedback on their learning.

By the time she went to her next job at a flagship state university, she was ready to take a deeper dive into her course design. First, she adjusted her assignments. Using the work she had done to identify the essential knowledge and skills her students needed to be successful in her field, she then worked to create lower stakes, formative assessments that would prepare students for her exams. She recognized that her practice of giving students 20-question problem sets ended up repeating concepts, but with diminishing returns. Feedback told her that students were anxious about completing the large problem sets, so she switched to 10-question problem sets to cover the same knowledge and skills and reduce the time pressure for her students. With fewer questions to answer, students spent more time on the concepts and became better prepared for exams. She wanted to make her pedagogy more transparent and to show students that she was committed to their success. She created a course map and "lesson plans" for every unit that included learning objectives, preparatory materials to support foundational concepts, aligned course learning outcomes, and learning assessments. She also made it clear to students that the problems she presented in class or in her problem sets would be the models for her exams. While exam questions could contain different values, students were assured that spending time and effort on this formative work would prepare them for high-stakes exams. Rather than simply delivering content, she wanted to ensure that all her students knew how to be successful in her courses and had the resources they needed.

As Katherine's experience shows, it's crucial for instructors to have a growth mindset toward their students, to believe that every student can achieve high standards. As a graduate student instructor, you might well teach students who don't seem as prepared or skilled as you were as an undergraduate. After all, graduate students often have the learning preferences, home lives, motivation, and foundational education that facilitate our success. This is why it may come as a shock when your students don't succeed under learning circumstances that worked for you. It can also be easy to see challenges in teaching as deficits in your students or in their educational backgrounds. A common refrain of many college educators seems to be "Why didn't they learn this in high school?" Funny enough, you can follow that question all the way down the ranks of K-12 ("Why didn't they learn this before my class?"). We might all wish to overhaul public education in the United States; however, until that glorious day, your teaching and the choices you make about it are much more within your control than large-scale educational policy revision. You also might be tempted to engage in the kind of informal student bashing that creates bonds with your colleagues through complaining. We get it—sometimes everyone needs to vent, but think twice before you begin your teaching practice from a position of complaint and deficit-minded condescension. As Kevin Gannon eloquently put it, "it's all too easy to critique novices for not being experts, even though when put in those stark terms, it's an absurd proposition" (2020, p. 42). Instead of lamenting your students' preparation, we encourage you to discover their strengths and potential.

To Katherine's credit, and a tribute to her training as a scientist, she was able to recognize the phenomena taking place in her classroom and to approach it as an intellectual puzzle, not as her own personal failing or as a deficit in her students. When she faced pushback from her students, she did not lower her standards in order to keep the peace, nor did she see lower student grades as evidence of her toughness and rigor. Instead, she took it upon herself to rethink her teaching methods.

Katherine knew that she wanted students to feel more confident with the concepts and succeed on her exams without making her course easier or removing important content that her students would need in later courses or in their professions. By determining what knowledge and skills were foundational to her course and what material was less necessary, she was able to focus her assignments and exams on what students needed most. Katherine was practicing backward design by starting with the big-picture goals and essential learning students needed from her course. She had been handed a course built on a coverage model, and had been educated in a similar way, but she was able to take a step back and construct her course around her students' learning. This process also gave her the chance to consider what evidence of student learning looked like. By requiring shorter problem sets, she was able to ensure that her students had mastered the material and provide them with more time to develop and test their understanding. Her transparent assignment and exam design also helped minimize student anxiety—and established a better rapport with her students. Students still needed to demonstrate their understanding of the concepts, but they now felt confident that class exercises and problem sets would prepare them for summative assessments like the exams. For lots of students, college feels like a game where others got the rules ahead of time. Katherine's changes helped to make the rules clearer, from the outset, for everyone.

Graduate students and new professors are often handed courses that have been designed in traditional coverage-model formats. We might presume that these familiar formats must be the best ways to teach the course. Frequently, we're told that students need to establish their foundational knowledge in a field before they can do more interesting work.

But how well does that approach work? Katherine's experiences helped her to identify that the traditional coverage model was actually a roadblock to her students' success. She could have blamed her students' initial lack of success on their lack of preparation, their lack of resources, or even their lack of motivation; after all, that was the perspective of others at her university. Instead, Katherine chose to assume that the students in her class could succeed. As we've said elsewhere, this doesn't mean reducing the learning in a course—it often means increasing deeper learning. As Katherine demonstrated, it means developing a growth mindset toward your students: believing that, with effort, students can succeed in your course and showing them the pathway.

Many of Katherine's strategies are explained in more detail in Chapter 2, especially in the sections on learner-centered course design and learning outcomes.

In our conversations with graduate instructors, some general themes emerged. One of the central themes is the importance of realizing that the students you teach may be very different from you. While it's a common, default move to complain about students, to see them as lacking in motivation, preparation, or intelligence, you can also take this opportunity to get to know your students and to believe in them. Sometimes, as in Edward's case, this optimism and determination comes from one's passion about the subject and a fierce belief that you can make the material matter to even nonmajors. In other cases, such as Ahmed's, you learn to recognize and check your assumptions about student behavior that puzzles or upsets you. Many of the graduate students above sought out advice from colleagues, chairs, and other mentors, and in doing so they began to treat teaching challenges as intellectual puzzles that require research, experimentation, and collaboration.

CHAPTER 8

CULTIVATING WELL-BEING

How are you supporting your well-being while you're in graduate school? Are there aspects of your life that you are holding off on pursuing until you graduate? Do you assume that you will have to isolate yourself and ignore your own well-being in order to be successful as a graduate student? Why? Where are you getting these messages? Both Aeron and Stephanie believed some version of these messages; however, they found creating community has been central to both their well-being and their success as academics. Sometimes the struggles we encounter are the impetus to creating community. For example, when Aeron was working on her PhD in literature, in the 1990s during the time of high theory, a graduate student's value seemed to depend upon the ease with which she could use abstruse post-structural philosophical terms. Since masters and PhD students took seminars together, this hierarchy became pronounced with a small number of experienced students dominating discussion. This was before the plethora of introductory theory books were published. Most folks responded to this pressure by hunkering down with their Lyotard and Derrida and reading and rereading dense passages until bits of coherence emerged. This is a necessary and productive strategy, but it didn't lessen the feeling of alienation and imposter syndrome that many experience. In response to feeling that they were being shut out of these discussions, a group of women graduate students started a theory reading group. It was revelatory for Aeron, who had taken a few years off before graduate school and was feeling unsure of her place, to see other smart, successful women graduate students struggling to comprehend and engage in the theory. The group served several purposes: first, it turned an isolating experience into a shared struggle. Second, it allowed women to practice engaging with theory without the presence of (often dominating) male voices and without worrying about performing for their professors and being judged. Eventually, it morphed into a feminist video production group that presented its collaborative work at a national conference. While this started as a community of learners, it evolved into a professional collaborative community; the group was able to realize far more potential together than simply gaining confidence with literary theory.

Even if you just started graduate school, you might also be looking for ways to ground what's happening in your teaching and course work in a larger framework or conversation. Ardon Shorr, a graduate student in biology at Carnegie Mellon University, formed a Public Communication for Researchers group with other graduate students in order to improve their ability to communicate science research to a wider audience: "The first thing we practiced was how to talk passionately about why we love research, what inspired us, what problem we're obsessed with" (Shorr, 2017). The strategies and goals of Shorr's group, Public Communication for Researchers, sound a lot like our recommendations for communicating your excitement and passion in the classroom. Although the group was primarily focused on communicating research to a lay audience, the workshops they built, speakers they engaged, and blog posts they wrote, all helped prepare these graduate students to break down complex subjects for nonexperts so that audiences could engage, ask questions, and understand the information—a great plan for learning. Shorr describes the ways in which the group felt empowered by working together to address a common need (feeling underprepared to communicate their research broadly) and how it positively affected his mental health. The group helped one another confront imposter syndrome by recognizing how similarly uncertain they all felt about their expertise, and they also came to realize that jargon-filled language can be a defensive posture for those trying to feign expertise.

As both accounts above show, forming community can help you combat the stress of graduate school and the imposter syndrome that strikes many graduate students. And, having some tools to combat stress and imposter syndrome will help you find the headspace to better put this book's strategies into practice.

Graduate school is challenging, even under the best of circumstances. Almost every one of the graduate students we interviewed for this book mentioned the stress they experienced in graduate school. The culture of graduate school has been described as "demoralizing" (Shorr, 2017), "dysfunctional . . . toxic" (Yesko, 2014), "lonely" and "a culture of critique" (Patterson, 2016), with a "hierarchy of power dynamics" ("5 Tips for Grad School Stress," 2018). A 2018 study of more than 2,000 graduate students in multiple disciplines across 234 institutions found that graduate students are "*more than six times* as likely to experience depression and anxiety as compared to the general population" (Evans et al.,

2018). (A later critique of that study's methods argues that graduate students are *only* 2.43 times more likely to experience mental health challenges (Duffy, Thanhouser, & Derry, 2019).) A study of economics graduate students across the US found that "18% of graduate students experience moderate or severe symptoms of depression and anxiety — more than three times the population average — and 11% report suicidal ideation in a two-week period" (Barreira, Basilico, & Bolotnyy, n.d.). A study of 387 psychology graduate students found that 68% of students reported that the demands of their graduate coursework were a pressure that moderately or significantly disrupted their lives (El-Ghoroury et al., 2012). The second highest stressor (at 63%) was financial, with anxiety listed third (60%) and poor work-life balance fourth (59%). "Burnout" was listed as a stressor by over 38% of students and a lack of professional support/isolation was felt by 36%. In a 2019 survey of graduate students at a public, research-intensive university with a high percentage of first-generation graduate students, 42% of respondents reported that mental health was a "minor obstacle" to their academic progress and 24% reported it as a "major obstacle" (Sanchez, 2019). More women than men in this study reported mental health as an obstacle (60% compared to 48%). Tellingly, students who have been in graduate school longer show *higher* rates of depression and anxiety. Graduate students of color face the compounding factors of institutional racism and negative interactions with health care professionals (Arday, 2018).

If you're struggling with anxiety, stress, or depression in graduate school, you are not alone, and it doesn't mean that you don't belong in academia. It will, however, impact your experience in graduate school and will affect your teaching. In this last chapter, we'd like to leave you with some strategies for taking care of yourself so that you can stay the course and so that you have the capacity to help your students thrive. In this chapter we are going to encourage you to prioritize your own well-being while in graduate school, to form collaborative teaching communities, and to find resources that can support and inspire you as you grow in your teaching practice.

Give Your Brain a Break

Graduate school often encourages a culture of hyperproductivity at the expense of quality of life. Although academia offers a greater degree of flexibility and autonomy compared to many other professions, this often comes at a cost: it's easy to feel that you're never really off the clock. When Aeron was writing her dissertation on Victorian literature, she pinned a quotation from Thomas Carlyle to her bulletin board:

> Produce! Produce! Were it but the pitifullest infinitesimal fraction of a product, produce it in God's name! 'Tis the utmost thou hast in thee; out with it then. Up, up! Whatsoever thy hand findeth to do, do it with thy whole might. Work while it is called To-day, for the Night cometh wherein no man can work. (1896 p. 187)

Carlyle's words crystalized Aeron's belief that the ideal graduate student spent all their time working and had no life outside of their studies. However, despite the single-minded, manic productivity described in that inspirational quotation, she rarely spent more than three solid hours writing her dissertation and still finished within one year. The rest of her day she spent reading, exercising, having meals with her roommates, and teaching. She found herself more productive when she had a more varied life than when she tried to monastically isolate herself with only work as a companion. While it is tempting to imagine that we can push ourselves to work nonstop by sheer determination and willpower, we have a limited capacity for mental focus. Very few people can work all day long at full productivity: "The idea that you can use 'grit' or 'self-control' to stay focused and productive every minute of every day is not merely incorrect, it's gaslighting, and it is potentially damaging to your brain" (Nagoski & Nagoski, 2019, p. 156). Our brains need time to recharge and so do our emotions and our bodies.

Whether you are a night owl or early bird, we suggest that you give yourself a regular schedule. If you've already worked an 8:00 to 5:00 job, you might be used to that routine or you might be ready to set something new. One of Stephanie's graduate school pals began each day walking her dog at 7:00, arrived on campus at 9:00, and worked or taught until 3:00, then she would take a break until 6:30 or 7:00 and do another hour or so of work before bed. Breaking up her day in this way ensured that she was making progress and keeping up with her teaching, but she wasn't so burned out from one day to the next. Also, consider what takes most of your energy and plan accordingly. If you get your best ideas later in the evening, maybe you dedicate that time to research and writing and save simpler tasks like answering emails for early in the day when your brain isn't quite awake.

Another strategy for giving your brain a break is to balance focus time with short breaks. A writing partner introduced Stephanie to the *Pomodoro Technique* in graduate school. The basics of the technique, developed by Francesco Cirillo, allow you to tackle one task at a time with short breaks to allow your brain to reset and maintain its stamina. A simple schedule would work like this:

- Work for 25 minutes on a single, focused task.
- Take a 5-minute break.
- Work for 25 minutes on a single, focused task.
- Take a 5-minute break.
- Work for 25 minutes on a single, focused task.
- Take a 5-minute break.
- Work for 25 minutes on a single, focused task.
- Take a 15-minute break.
- Repeat!

Those 25 minutes of work could be small chunks of the same work, like grading or writing, or they could be separate tasks, like marking off items on your to-do list. When you are facing something daunting, or feeling your motivation lag, it can be helpful to tell yourself you only have to do it for 25 minutes. Often, after the initial 25 minutes you become engaged in the task.

Give Your Body a Break

Our minds and bodies are connected. The foundations of physical wellness are not surprising or controversial: you need to sleep, eat, and move your body. This may seem like common sense, but it can feel revolutionary when you're a graduate student to treat yourself with care and factor in physical health to your long list of intellectual priorities. It's not surprising that research shows how sleep improves cognitive functioning and memory (Ellenbogen et al., 2006) and that a lack of sleep impacts your mood (van der Helm & Walker, 2009) as well as your physical health. Are any of us the best versions of ourselves without a good night's rest? Most adults need at least seven hours of sleep each night (Watson et al., 2015). Although some people can function on less sleep for a period, a lack of this basic physical need will have repercussions.

Nutritional psychiatry also demonstrates how the food that we eat affects our moods (Lai et al., 2014). As Sarris et al. argue in *The Lancet*, we are now living in a time when people are often consuming "nutrient-poor, energy-dense, highly processed food" that leaves us "overfed and undernourished" (Sarris et al., 2015). Studies have found eating processed foods high in sugar can be harmful to your brain's functioning as well as your moods. What can you do? Pay attention to what you eat and notice how you feel after eating certain foods. Notice how you feel when you don't eat. Even if you don't think of yourself as someone who likes to cook, the process of preparing a nourishing meal for yourself can provide a calming break from abstract intellectual labor. Cooking a family recipe can also be a way to connect to your home even if you're far away.

We all know that movement is important for our physical health, but it also helps us manage stress. Physical movement is an important way that humans have responded to extreme stress (Nagoski & Nagoski, 2019). Our bodies' primitive response to threats involved physical action like running, fighting, or even shaking after the threat ended. Unfortunately, our bodies can react to modern-day stresses, such as hostile email, upsetting political news, public humiliation, or even traffic, as if they were physically life threatening. We often fail to "complete the stress cycle" with physical action; instead we ruminate, worry, and carry the stress around in our bodies and minds, which can cause high blood pressure, weakened immune systems, and increased anxiety. Is stress always harmful? Not necessarily. The nervousness you feel before an important presentation, when meeting your students for the first time, or before a job interview can give you increased energy and focus. Some research suggests that *how we think about* the stress we experience can influence its effect on us (McGonigal, 2016). For example, if our heart rate increases slightly as we approach the classroom, this is a stress response but could be reframed as excitement to help us bring our passion to the classroom. Whether your own stress feels invigorating or overwhelming, it helps to work it out through physical activity.

Some of you may already do this by running, biking, practicing martial arts, or engaging in other cardiovascular exercise regularly. Aeron's husband, a therapist, knows that he needs at least three intense bike rides every week in order to regulate the stress that his job involves. Stephanie found a few other graduate students to swim with at the campus pool three times a week during her master's program. They met during lunchtime and motivated each other to swim for 20–30 minutes before they ate their packed lunches. It doesn't have to be a major investment of time: a brisk walk around campus or even a series of progressive relaxation exercises can allow you to complete the stress cycle. Research also suggests that sex with a partner and physical affection can lower blood pressure and help people recover from stressful situations (Burleson, Trevathan, & Todd, 2006). There is also some research indicating that pets can reduce stress levels (Miller et al., 2009). Pay attention to the somatic responses you are having in your daily life so that you can take note of when you need to complete the stress cycle.

Give Yourself a Break

Many graduate students will face moments when their confidence falters. As a first-year master's student, Aeron was in seminars with advanced PhD students who seemed intimidatingly fluent in the language of post-structural theory. Aeron had taken two years off between college and graduate school and her academic writing skills were rusty. At a time when she felt least confident about her own academic writing, she was teaching freshman composition, a course she had never taken. She felt like a fraud. In her six years of graduate school, her skills as a writer, reader, and teacher increased, but she never quite shook the feeling that she was faking it, that she really didn't know what she was doing. Ironically, the summer before Aeron began graduate school, a woman professor and friend of the family warned her that women often experience something called imposter syndrome when in graduate school. Aeron dismissed the warning because she had been a very confident and high-achieving college student. Years later, she remembered the comment and wondered if what she experienced in graduate school was a common phenomenon. *Imposter syndrome*, the feeling that one is a fraud despite evidence to the contrary, can strike any of us and can make us feel like we don't belong. It thrives in certain contexts, such as "communities with arbitrary, unnecessary standards, where harsh criticism is the norm, and where secrecy surrounds the actual process [of accomplishments]" (Gardiner & Aurora, 2013). Sounds a lot like grad school, right?

Those experiencing imposter syndrome often either over-prepare or procrastinate because of anxiety and self-doubt. Those who overprepare will think their success is predicated on their excess work (Sakulku, 2011, p. 78). Those who procrastinate may think that any good fortune is just luck. Imposter syndrome thrives in graduate school because of the unspoken norms, attitudes, and skills (or hidden curriculum) that are not explicitly taught but are expected. For example, how do you build a mentoring relationship with a professor? What should you do if members of your dissertation committee hate each other? Who do you talk to when your teaching isn't going well? Even the fundamental academic skills required in graduate school are rarely made explicit. Recently on Twitter there was a popular thread, "Stuff graduate students are too often expected to learn how to do by magic." The list included publish academic articles, teach, navigate the job market, navigate academic conferences, develop a research proposal, conduct a peer review, fulfill administrative duties, and translate skills to nonacademic jobs. In a competitive, scarcity-based culture, there is a lot of pressure to appear confident and knowledgeable. Admitting that you're struggling or unsure of yourself is scary when you need your professors and your department to invest in you.

Imposter syndrome isn't a failure of self-confidence—it's often a response to the way individuals are treated and the implicit and explicit messages they receive from their environment. While imposter syndrome was first used to explain why white, middle- or upper-middle-class high-achieving women had trouble internalizing their achievements and successes (Clance & Imes, 1978), more recent research suggests that women of color and those who are the first in their families to attend college experience imposter syndrome at higher levels and more often (Canning et al., 2019; Patterson-Stephens, Lane, & Vital, 2017). Remember Maria's reflection from our Introduction? A high-achieving student her whole life, she was recognized as an excellent student in tangible ways. However, once in graduate school she was one of the only women of color and one of the few students from the area. She often heard faculty and fellow graduate students comment on the lack of preparedness of the program's undergraduates, students who looked like her and went to high schools similar to her own. She began to doubt herself and her place in the program. Sindhumathi Revuluri, associate dean of undergraduate education at Harvard, argues, "some academics don't just feel like imposters, they are *made* to feel like imposters, no matter how self-assured, smart, and confident they are" (Revuluri, 2018). Revuluri's essay on how to combat imposter syndrome offers useful advice for everyone but may be particularly necessary for graduate students from minoritized groups:

- Learn to see yourself in context: when you are brand new to teaching, don't expect that you will have all the same know-how or confidence as someone who has been teaching for a few semesters.
- Avoid false comparisons: it took years (even decades) for your advisors to get to where they are in their careers. That work may have taken place in a vastly different job market than the one you are facing. Their success doesn't have to be your aim.
- Acknowledge the additional stress of being the only person from your background/identity in a program.
- Create your own "board of advisors" to support and guide you. (Revuluri, 2018).

These strategies can provide you a much-needed reality check when you aren't feeling like your best professional self, or when the people around you aren't acknowledging that you are still learning the profession.

Revuluri's last piece of advice can be one of the most effective ways to combat imposter syndrome and to increase your mental health: form community and seek out mentors. Graduate school—and academia as a whole—is structured to be a solitary, competitive endeavor. Individual accomplishments are prized, and collaboration is rarely valued.

Resources and jobs are scarce, which often results in a tendency to see others as competitors, not collaborators and allies. However, having connections and forming communities is vital to our ability to thrive: Nagoski and Nagoski explain, "Connection nourishes us in a literal, physical way, regulating our heart rates and respiration rates, influencing the emotional activation in our brains, shifting our immune response to injuries and wounds, changing our exposure to stressors, and modulating our stress response" (Nagoski & Nagoski, 2019, p. 134). Studies have shown that social connection can help us build resilience in the face of stressful situations. A now-famous study conducted at the University of Washington challenged the theory that everyone reacts to stress with a fight-or-flight response. UW researchers found that many women (and some men) react to stress by "tending and befriending" or by caring for others and creating community (Taylor et al., 2000). The communities that we form are necessary supports.

While having community within your program can prevent you from feeling isolated by the experiences of graduate school, having community outside of your cohort can also help you see yourself (and your stress) in a broader context. By pure luck, Stephanie had roommates outside of her program for most of graduate school. Her first roommate was from the local area and had a large group of friends from her undergraduate mountaineering club. These people introduced her to local hiking trails and camping spots. They gave her a used bike for commuting (and taught her to ride it when she had to embarrassingly admit that she had forgotten how to ride a bike!). Through her roommate, she met professionals across the city who worked in engineering, laser optics, nutrition, public relations and marketing, public health, and physical therapy. When a committee member declined to see Stephanie through her master's thesis, or when she had to push her comprehensive exams back a semester, knowing people in different fields who had struggled gave her a lot of perspective. For example, there was the engineer who had gotten Cs in front-door math courses, a nutritionist who had to completely reconceptualize her thesis at the last minute because of Institutional Review Board difficulties, and quite a few medical professionals who didn't get into their program the first time but who went on to be successful in their fields.

In addition to forming communities, consider adopting a "network-mentor model" (Rockquemore, 2011; Janasz & Sullivan, 2004; Sorcinelli & Yun, 2007) in which you *identify specific needs* and then seek out mentors who have experience in these areas. These can be very wide-ranging, such as how to apply for a grant, how to teach a course, how to handle microaggressions from a faculty member, how to tailor your job letter for a small liberal arts college, or feedback on your writing, etc. Faculty developer Kerry Ann Rockquemore argues against the traditional "guru model" of mentoring in which one faculty member meets all a graduate student's needs. Often, this type of mentoring relationship results in the mentor attempting to form the mentee into a miniaturized version of themselves, instead of responding to the specific needs of the graduate student. Instead, meet your needs with a variety of resources. Does your campus have a graduate center that offers dissertation support groups? Are there any existing support structures on your campus for graduate students of color? Are there online support groups that would connect you with folks in similar situations outside of your institution? Stephanie spent a year going to every week-long writing boot camp offered by her graduate resource center to make it through her dissertation. Aeron was part of a Victorian studies dissertation writing group organized by her dissertation director, Professor Elizabeth Langland. When Stephanie was starting to have doubts about the academic job market, she talked to professors outside her committee who were more open to alternative academic careers and she saw a therapist who specialized in working with women. We encourage you to seek out any support that your university provides, including individual therapy, and it's OK to pick and choose who is going to meet your individual needs. We also strongly recommend that you identify a support or mentoring group for yourself. You don't have to do graduate school alone, and we strongly advise against it.

It might help to connect your graduate work with a larger purpose. In what ways do you hope that your research will benefit society? Reminding yourself of the larger purpose of your work, instead of focusing on your individual achievements, has been shown to increase persistence and lessen stress (McGonigal, 2016, p. 151). Seeing your own struggles as in service of a larger goal may help combat the isolation that graduate work can engender. In addition to the larger contributions your research will make, consider the profound impact that your teaching can have on hundreds of students. You have a greater impact than you recognize. You may not ever realize how your small acts of generosity affected certain students or how you modeled the values of your discipline for others.

It is tempting—and sometimes encouraged—to delay taking care of yourself until you're done with graduate school. Please don't do this! It is a myth that you can separate intellectual labor from physical and mental health. Graduate school is too long a process to ignore your health and well-being and postponing living a healthy life can become a pernicious habit. If you're lucky enough to get a tenure-track job, you'll be encouraged to postpone everything but research until after tenure, then until after you get that big grant or publish your monograph, then until after you achieve a promotion to full professor—rinse and repeat ad nauseum. It is a myth that your life will magically transform once you become a professor. The CEO and founder of Beyond the Professoriate, L. Maren Wood, is in the process of conducting a survey on graduate students and those who have received their PhDs in the past seven years, hypothesizing that depression and anxiety persists past graduation due to the severe "career uncertainty" that many PhDs face (Wood, 2020). Moreover, the high rates of burnout among the professoriate make it clear that the stress of an academic lifestyle doesn't resolve itself after you land a full-time job or even tenure (Lackritz, 2004; Watts & Robertson, 2011). Instead, address these challenges now and start to build the habits you want to have as an educator—for the benefit of your students and yourself. The academy will never tell you that you've done enough, nor will it reward your single-minded devotion by giving you a full and happy life. And in the meantime, you have missed opportunities to develop a joyful, sustainable life, one that can support a rewarding teaching practice.

Wellness might seem an odd way to conclude a book about college teaching. However, ignoring your emotional and physical health can impact the way you teach, damage your own success as a graduate student, and limit your teaching effectiveness. If you are struggling with chronic stress or overwhelming anxiety, this needs to be addressed first. When we experience chronic anxiety or depression, we are less able to be thoughtful teachers; at worst, we unwittingly dump our own stress and toxicity onto our students. Graduate students are in the unique position of being in the middle of the academic hierarchy and there is a tendency to enact oppressive experiences on the people beneath you in the power dynamic, namely, the students.[13] Good teaching is grounded in compassionate understanding of our students—their complicated lives and individual struggles—so it makes sense to begin with some compassion toward yourselves.

APPENDIX 1

HELP! WHAT IF MY COURSE STARTS NEXT WEEK?

If you were given a section of a course that began a week from now, where would you go for advice and resources? Ideally, you would have at least a semester to prepare for a new course. This gives you time to research, consult with others, plan, reflect, and refine your course plan. Unfortunately, most universities are beholden to swings in enrollment and you might find yourself in the position of having to prepare to teach a course given very little notice. For example, while in graduate school, Stephanie and Aeron were both assigned sections of courses at the last minute as the result of instructor shortages or personal emergencies. Other times, you'll need to redesign your course due to some unplanned disruption: natural disasters (becoming more and more common each year) or other regional and national crises may mean that even your best laid plans will need to change. During the 2020-2021 COVID-19 health crisis, instructors everywhere were asked to redesign the remainder of their spring semester courses with just one- or two-weeks' notice—and, in some instances, that one week was also spring break. So, what do you do when you must design or redesign a course in a hurry?

It's difficult for everyone when you are asked to teach a course (or make a major change) last minute, but it doesn't mean that the students registered for that course don't deserve a positive learning experience. This is where a triage approach can be helpful. Below we've given you a checklist that draws from the strategies outlined in the rest of this book to help you move through planning for a course quickly and efficiently, prioritizing what needs to happen before the semester begins and knowing that you will be doing additional planning as the term progresses. Depending on the level of flexibility your department allows, you might be working with prescribed material or you may have a lot of room to create your own plan. Having lots of prescribed material can be helpful and keep you from spending too much time building from scratch, but it can also be frustrating if you are feeling hemmed in. You may have more ownership than you think, so pay attention to the key questions below that will help you determine what needs to be used, and what is optional.

Before the Semester Begins (One–Two Weeks)

Assess What You Have

✓ Gather and review any available materials from your department, colleagues, or the course catalogue. These may include the following:
- Course descriptions.
- Required course outcomes.
- A syllabus template, if one is available. If not, what are the mandated syllabus components (e.g., accessibility statement, academic integrity statement, etc.)?
- Copies of the required texts if they have already been ordered.

✓ Ask your department or colleagues what kinds of students

typically enroll in the course. Are these majors, nonmajors, or both? Is the course a general education requirement?

- ✓ Ask colleagues for example assignments. This will help you norm your workload.
- ✓ If applicable, determine what mandated work students may need to do to complete the course (e.g., Aeron and Stephanie both taught in Florida where certain courses require a specific number of college-level writing assignments).
- ✓ Determine your own limitations in time or resources for the semester.
  - When are your own seminar papers, grants, or conference submissions due?
  - What religious holidays or family/caregiver obligations will you need to block out time for?

Determine What Can Be Used and What Can Be Changed

If you have gathered all the available materials and you are still feeling like the guidance is minimal, don't worry. The fewer guidelines and requirements the course has, the more freedom you will have to make the course your own. Your next step is to determine what can be changed and what you'd like to change. If possible, consider the following:

- ✓ Rephrase the learning outcomes or course description in your own language. This will help you to explain it clearly to students. If you need to use required language, can you frame it within your own explanation?
- ✓ If the course text(s) isn't your choice, what parts would you be comfortable using. If students have already been instructed to purchase the text(s), it's not a good idea to ditch the resource wholesale. Students will feel like they've wasted their money. What can you supplement with no additional cost from your library or from other high-quality sources?

Build What You Need

✓ Draft an inclusive syllabus using the checklist below, or syllabus templates required by your department. You'll want the language to be learner-centered and for it to communicate to your students that they belong in your course.

- Learning outcomes: measurable and written in learner-centered language. For examples, see Chapter 2.
- Contact information for you and your department.
- A description of the course written in novice-friendly language.
- A list of required materials.
- Community expectations and classroom norms. Explain what steps a student will need to take to be successful in your course and how you expect them to participate and collaborate. This section should include a statement from you or your university in which you commit to creating an inclusive and welcoming environment in your course. Ask students to communicate with you if something you are doing, or something happening in the class, is preventing their success. You can also use the activity from Chapter 3 to co-create this section of the syllabus with your students.
- Grading policies, attendance/participation expectations, and guidelines for academic integrity.
- Campus or community resources that might support students struggling in your course.
- Accessibility resources: who should a student talk to and how can they get help?

(Adapted from UCLA's and Vanderbilt's Inclusive Syllabus Checklist, https://ceils.ucla.edu/resources/teaching-guides/syllabus-design/; see also https://provost.tufts.edu/celt/files

/Inclusion-by-Design-Survey-Your-Syllabus-Brantmeier-Broscheid-Moore-1.pdf)

- ✓ Determine major projects or assignments and build these into a semester calendar. Add semester breaks, campus closures, and important dates like the last day to drop the course without incurring a cost.
- ✓ Plan your first week in detail:
  - How will you welcome students to the course?
  - How will you perform your enthusiasm for this topic?
  - What activities will help you learn about your students? (An easy way to do this is to have students share their previous experience with topics that will be covered in a course. For example, in an exercise science course on teaching motor skills the instructor might ask students to share with one another a time in which they were taught a motor skill in an effective way.)
  - What activities will help you create community within the classroom? These could overlap with the activities that help you learn about your students, but they can also be complementary. Can students form project groups based on topics of interest? Can students form study groups?
  - Decide if you will give students an opportunity to influence the trajectory of the course, and how you will let them know this in the first week. For example, can students choose one supplemental text or reading? Can students choose their own topic for a project or assignment?
- ✓ Build in feedback loops:
  - Determine how you will give students regular, substantive feedback on their progress toward the course learning outcomes. These can be low-stakes assignments that let students know how they're doing in the course.

Once you have identified your formative assessments, use that and any required materials to complete your course calendar.

- Schedule a time during the semester when you will collect anonymous feedback from your students. We recommend somewhere between a third and halfway through the semester. You can use or adapt the sample questions in Chapter 4, "Checking in and Getting Feedback." Or, you could ask your campus teaching center to conduct a mid-semester feedback session with your students.

Once the Semester Begins

Week by Week

When you have very little time to plan, it's likely that you will be building the course week by week. This is ok. You can still plan for engaging and inclusive learning experiences if you follow the steps below, on repeat.

✓ Plan your upcoming week by determining the answers to the following:
- What will students need to do to make progress on their formative assignments or their major projects? What can they practice together, what can you model for them?
- What supplements and examples will you need to build for them to do this work?
- Is there optional choice or autonomy you can build into the next week's activities?

✓ Reflect on the past week. It can be helpful to keep these notes in a single journal or even jot them down directly on your syllabus.
- What went well, and what did you feel was missing?

- Which of your learning outcomes are students struggling with? Which skills or understandings have they already demonstrated mastery over? If it's clear that your entire class has mastered one of your course learning outcomes, can you cut some assignments to make more time for practicing something they're struggling with?
- How are you communicating that struggling students still belong in the course? What can you do to help them catch up and move ahead?

The Final Week

You'll want to plan your final week to help students reflect on the progress they've made, imagine what's possible for them moving forward, and provide you with useful feedback for the next time you teach the course.

- ✓ How will the class identify and celebrate the progress you've made together? See the Chapter 4 section on "Celebrating Progress" for ideas to help you plan your final class.
- ✓ Does your department use a mandated student evaluation and are there certain questions that will give you more valuable feedback than others? Make sure students know how you plan to use their evaluations. If your department does not use an evaluation form that you find useful, consider adding your own reflective evaluation in the final week that will give you the feedback you need. Be sure to make the feedback anonymous otherwise you may not get the candid feedback you want.
- ✓ What can you share with students that will kindle further interest in the course's topic? Are there community opportunities for them in this area, are there national or international forums appropriate for undergraduates that they can join?

After the Semester Ends

Once your grades are turned in and your seminar papers submitted, take a breath. You did it! Take a moment to review the journal or notes you kept throughout the term. What were your major victories? How did your students surprise you and what did you learn from their work? What didn't work? Was it due to poor planning, poor execution, or simply a bad idea? (We have all had a few of those.) Make a couple of big-picture decisions and jot these down on your syllabus so you can quickly reference when you teach the course again. Once you have access to your student evaluations or the reflective work you asked students to produce, read through their comments once and summarize them. Be wary of fixating on the one or two negative remarks. Instead, compare the notes you made on the syllabus to your students' responses to the course. Are there any major differences between what you thought was successful about the course and what students thought worked well? There might be an assignment you thought went well, but they didn't find purpose in. Select a couple of concrete suggestions made by students to improve the course. Add these to your notes on the syllabus and consider how you will tell your future students that you have incorporated previous students' feedback in designing the course.

APPENDIX 2

HOW CAN MY TEACHING EXPERIENCE HELP ME GET A JOB?

How do you demonstrate to a hiring committee that you're an effective teacher? It's not enough to show that you have had *experience* teaching, you will also need to convince the hiring committee that you are committed and knowledgeable about teaching. In this Appendix we're going to help you think about how you will communicate your experience, your teaching skills, and your approach to teaching in a short statement that is called a "statement of teaching philosophy" or "teaching statement." We'll also help you plan for an on-campus teaching demonstration, which can be a nerve-racking part of the interview process. Whether you're aiming to teach at a research-intensive university, a small liberal arts college, a regional comprehensive, or a community college, being able to show a search committee that you will be a strong teacher is increasingly important.

A teaching philosophy or teaching statement is a short narrative document (generally one–two pages) that you often submit when you apply for a position as assistant professor or for a graduate teaching award. In a survey of 457 search committee members in different disciplines (English, history, political science, psychology, biology, and chemistry) and types of institutions, "91.5% of respondents ranked teaching ability as important or very important to the academic hiring process" (Meizlish & Kaplan, 2008). Of all the things we write professionally as academics, the teaching philosophy is probably the most personal and reflective in tone. As a result, this can be a perplexing part of the job application process for many graduate students. Aeron has been on numerous search committees for assistant professors, and she's read hundreds of teaching statements. Most sound eerily similar; few really give the search committee a sense of the applicant's strengths or potential as a teacher. You don't want your teaching statement to be too general; instead, your statement is your chance to highlight your specific teaching strengths and to show your commitment to an ongoing practice. Below is one way to approach writing your statement that Aeron has used with her graduate students.

The Moves of the Discipline

(This is the first paragraph of your teaching statement)

You've spent a substantial part of your life devoted to your field. What do you see as the unique ways that your discipline makes sense of the world? This is a giant, difficult question, but you have already wrestled with it in Chapter 2 on course design. Begin your teaching philosophy with a succinct statement articulating the value of your discipline. For example, an historian might write, "I want my students to realize that history is not what is found in a textbook, it is a constantly evolving argument about the past, one that they have the power to shape." Often, statements focus more on the writer's own educational journey and not the ways that the writer has guided students to make these discoveries.

Show, Not Tell

(These are your second and third paragraphs of your teaching statement)

In the previous paragraph you've communicated a large, aspirational goal. Next, let the reader see you in action: describe a specific assignment or exercise that demonstrates how you have helped students recognize the value of your discipline. It's not enough to list the content you assign; explain one specific way that you make the material come alive for students. For example, a historian might describe how her student read conflicting accounts of an historical event, such as the Sand Creek Massacre of 1864, and how they made sense of these multiple perspectives on a single historical event. Consider including examples of how your students responded to your assignments, the ways that they surprised you, as well as the specific innovations you created.

Let your specific assignment illustrate your teaching practice. Do you believe strongly in undergraduate research, writing to learn, or collaborative work? Then show how you employ these methods. For example, in her teaching philosophy statement, Stephanie describes an assignment where students reading Homer's *The Odyssey* create a class wiki for a future cohort that explains difficult concepts, helps them keep characters and locations straight, and helps them work collaboratively on a multimodal project. This shows that she values students co-creating knowledge in her courses, formative writing to learn, and that she can create authentic assessments that ground students' work in a real-life need. What assignment are you most proud of or do you use most often? Did you use the assignment or exercise again and, if so, what kind of tweaks did you perform to make it more successful? Paint a picture for the search committee of your classroom practice. Make sure to include examples of how you've adapted your courses to different modalities, if you have. If you aren't sure where to start on this, go back through student feedback from previous terms and look at your student evaluations and any reflective writing you did about your course. What did students find most helpful and memorable about your teaching?

Plans to Develop as a Teacher

(This is the fourth paragraph of your teaching statement)

Nobody expects a new PhD to have all the answers about teaching. One of the best ways to show how committed you are to teaching is to recognize and acknowledge what you *don't* know and where you need to grow. If you haven't been given a chance to create your own course yet, describe a course you plan to develop in your field. What material do you want to build or what content would you like to incorporate? Mention any teaching workshops, teaching articles, teaching sites, or teaching mentors that have influenced your thinking about teaching.

If you are doing graduate work at an institution whose population more closely mirrors the general population (such as an Hispanic Serving Institution, Historically Black College or University, or an institution that enrolls many first-generation college students), then you have a leg up on colleagues who have been teaching only at private, wealthy, or predominantly white institutions. Show the committee that you know how to establish and cultivate a welcoming learning environment that leverages the most effective strategies for supporting all students. How have you enacted these strategies in your courses, and what are you continuing to learn to improve them? For those of you who haven't had the opportunity to teach a more representative population, we recommend you draw on strategies outlined in Chapters 3 and 4 to start planning how you will teach more inclusively. In a rubric on inclusive teaching philosophies from the University of Michigan, excellence is demonstrated by the following: "Portrays a coherent philosophy of inclusive education that is integrated throughout the statement. Discussion of roles is sensitive to historically under-represented students. Demonstrates awareness of issues of equity within the discipline" (Kaplan, et al., 2005). If no one is talking to you about this in your department, you may need to seek out discipline-specific resources and mentors to help you develop your strategies. We also suggest that you take advantage of the readings listed in Appendix 3. Clearly articulate what actions you take to make your classroom welcoming and accessible for all students.

Revising and Tailoring Your Statement

Have a few different mentors and colleagues read your statement. If you have a graduate writing center on your campus, get some feed-back from them as well. You don't have to take every piece of advice offered, but it will give you a variety of perspectives to consider. An easy way to quickly tailor your statement to a particular institution is to look at your plans to develop as an instructor and address how those plans will benefit that department, their programs, or their students. For example, if you are applying to a math department that has an in-house peer tutoring, you might address how you want to leverage those resources in your course design. In Appendix 3, we also list websites with examples of statements from different disciplines.

Preparing for an On-Campus Teaching Demo

When you become a finalist for an academic position, you may be asked to give a teaching demonstration in addition to a talk on your research, or, in some instances in place of the traditional research talk. The teaching demonstration is one of the most challenging and high-stakes teaching situations you will encounter. Even after years of experience and numerous teaching awards, Aeron and Stephanie were both very nervous when they prepared for their on-campus teaching demos. The campus setting is probably new to you and you haven't had a chance to build rapport with the class. However, the search committee selected you because they believe that you are a strong candidate. Most likely, they read your teaching statement and they want to see the principles/approaches you described there.

The search committee is looking to see that the students understand and are engaged with the material. Committees (and students) want to see confidence and enthusiasm. This is an opportunity for you to demonstrate your own teaching strengths: do not attempt to create some entirely new persona or use an untried method. The teaching demo is also a chance to find out more about the students at the institution. A teaching demonstration typically occurs in one of two environments: either you will be asked to teach an existing class or you will be asked to present to a mock class composed of a mixed group of faculty and students. Even when you are guest lecturing in an existing course, members of the search committee will usually attend and take notes. Try to ignore them as much as you can and focus on the students.

Be clear about the committee's expectations. It's perfectly reasonable to ask the search committee questions, like the ones listed below, that will help you prepare for this demonstration:

- How many students are enrolled in the class?
- Are the students mostly majors or nonmajors?
- What is the layout and technology in the room?
- Is the building's wifi reliable?
- Are the students used to a lecture or discussion format?
- May you have a copy of the course syllabus?
- Would it be appropriate to contact the instructor of the course so that you can tailor your lesson to their course goals?

- Will the students complete a survey on your teaching? If so, can you have a copy so that you understand the committee's goals?

If you're asked to teach a preassigned topic, do your best to research it thoroughly and get a sense of where the topic fits into the larger course goals. The search committee often wants to see if you can teach outside the narrow area of your dissertation. If you are asked to pick your own topic or if the search committee specifically asks you to teach your dissertation topic, think very carefully about how you will make it understandable and relevant to a nonexpert. Keep in mind that your goal here is to show the committee how you can engage their students, it is not to impress experts in your field.

It's a safe bet to plan a lesson that is a mix of you talking and the students doing something. Refer to the sample class plans in Chapter 4 to see an outline that might be helpful. Don't plan your lesson around the expectation that the students will have reviewed the material ahead of time. If your teaching demo plan requires feedback from the students and no one responds, you will be in an awkward situation. One smart strategy is to build in a mini lecture that gives everyone in the room a clearer sense of the material. You can also bring in a short handout or primary source that allows you to examine the concepts together.

- Make sure your handouts are clear and that you print them ahead of time.
- If you plan to use technology, make sure you have a backup for anything pivotal, such as transcripts of a video or materials on a thumb drive or in a cloud drive.
- Briefly introduce yourself.
- Tell them your topic and give them a reason to care about it.
- Make sure that any activity directions are clear (and relatively uncomplicated).

- Make eye contact and smile.
- When a student offers a comment, thank them and rephrase the comment to make sure you understand them and so that everyone can hear them.
- Formulate questions ahead of time to ask students.
- Conclude with a summary of the discussion (if there was one) or end with a reminder of how this topic connects to their course goals.
- Thank them and invite them to continue the conversation after class.
- Do not make assumptions about your audience. Be careful relying on humor that assumes a shared context or set of beliefs.
- Do not use unfamiliar technology or a brand new teaching strategy: this will create unnecessary stress and will not allow your teaching strengths to shine.
- Do not fill your slides (if you are using them) with small text, images, or graphs.

Above all, *practice* your teaching demo. Ask a group of friends to be your audience. Go through your planned lesson several times until it feels natural and fluid. Time yourself. Practice what you will do if many students respond and if no student responds to your questions.

Keep in mind that most students are generous to guests and will try their best to help you out. A teaching demo doesn't have to be perfect to get you the job. Aeron remembers one unpleasant on-campus interview where she was asked to teach an 8:00 a.m. class. The students were unresponsive no matter how animated she tried to be. What made it even worse was that every time she told a joke the search committee members who were sitting in the back guffawed loudly while the students sat stone-faced. It was one of her least inspiring teaching experiences, but she was offered the job. Stephanie once prepared a teaching demo that relied on the audience being able to view a short video speech at the outset. She had planned ahead enough to bring transcripts of the speech for the audience, but her activity on rhetorical strategies was meant to be paired with the video presentation of the speech. When the classroom speakers failed, she quickly pivoted to having the audience take turns reading through the speech. They still offered her the position and made a point to note that the technology failure was on their end. Often your ability to bounce back after glitches impresses the committee as much as a flawless performance.

APPENDIX 3

RESOURCES

The first resource we encourage you to check out is your campus teaching and learning center. Most centers will have workshops open to graduate students on a variety of topics, robust websites, and many offer confidential consultations.

Centers for Teaching and Learning Websites with Helpful Resources

Vanderbilt's Center for Teaching: A useful set of "guides" for many teaching topics, such as "difficult dialogues," "the first day," "group work," "office hours," and many more; *https://cft.vanderbilt.edu*

The University of Calgary's Taylor Institute for Teaching and Learning: Resources on the scholarship of teaching and learning as well as a resource page on Indigenous Ways of Knowing; https://taylorinstitute.ucalgary.ca

Blogs and Podcasts about College Teaching

Dead Ideas in Teaching and Learning: A series that debunks the common misconception about teaching and learning; hosted by

Catherine Ross at Columbia University's Center for Teaching and Learning; https://ctl.columbia.edu/resources-and-technology/resources/podcast/

Tea for Teaching: A series of informal discussions of innovative and effective practices in teaching and learning hosted by John Kane and Rebecca Mushtare. John and Rebecca run the Center for Excellence in Learning and Teaching at the State University of New York at Oswego; http://teaforteaching.com

Teaching in Higher Ed: This podcast is hosted by Bonni Stachowiak, a professor of business and management and dean of teaching and learning at Vanguard University of Southern California. Each week Bonni interviews leaders in the field of teaching and learning and digital pedagogy. She also includes strategies for productivity and organization; https://teachinginhighered.com/

Tomorrow's Professor: This online newsletter is published twice weekly by Richard M. Reis at Stanford University. It highlights recent research and often contains an excerpt from a new book or article on teaching; https://tomprof.stanford.edu/welcome

Cult of Pedagogy: Several topics that provide excellent introductions to big concepts in teaching like active learning, learning theory, or incorporating technology; https://www.cultofpedagogy.com/blog/

Hybrid Pedagogy: Articles and recordings on topics ranging from critical digital pedagogy to pedagogies of care and un-grading; https://hybridpedagogy.org/

Publications

Learning Science

Ambrose, S., Bridges, M., & Lovett, M. (2010). *How learning works: 7 research-based principles for smart teaching*. John Wiley and Sons.

Brown, P. C., Roediger, H. L., III, & McDaniel, M. A. (2014). *Make it stick: The science of successful learning*. Belknap/Harvard.

Cavanagh, S. R. (2016). *The spark of learning: Energizing the college classroom with the science of emotion*. West Virginia University Press.

Eyler, J. R. (2018). *How humans learn: The science and stories behind effective college teaching*. West Virginia University Press.

Hammond, Z. (2015). *Culturally responsive teaching and the brain: Promoting authentic engagement and rigor among culturally and linguistically diverse students*. Corwin.

Verschelden, C. (2017). *Bandwidth recovery: helping students reclaim cognitive resources lost to poverty, racism, and social marginalization*. Stylus.

Zull, J. E. (2002). *The art of changing the brain: Enriching the practice of teaching by exploring the biology of learning*. Stylus.

College Teaching

Brookfield, S. D., & Preskill, S. (2012). *Discussion as a way of teaching: Tools and techniques for democratic classrooms*. Wiley.

Fink, L. D. (2013). *Creating significant learning experiences: An integrated approach to designing college courses*. Jossey-Bass.

Gannon, K. M. (2020). *Radical hope: A teaching manifesto*. West Virginia University Press.

Gooblar, D. (2019). *The missing course: Everything they never taught you about college teaching*. Harvard University Press.

hooks, b. (1994) *Teaching to transgress*. Routledge.

Lang, J. M. (2016). *Small teaching: Everyday lessons from the science of learning*. Jossey-Bass.

Middendorf, J., & Shopkow, L. (2018). *Overcoming student learning bottlenecks*. Stylus.

Neuhaus, J. (2019). *Geeky pedagogy: A guide for intellectuals, introverts, and nerds who want to be effective teachers*. West Virginia University Press.

Richmond, A. S., Boysen, G. A., & Gurung, R. A. (2016). *An evidence-based guide to college and university teaching: Developing the model teacher*. Routledge.

Higher Education

Cassuto, L. (2015). *The graduate school mess*. Harvard University Press.
Davidson, C. (2017). *The new education: How to revolutionize the university to prepare students for a world in flux*. Hachett.
Tough, P. (2019). *The inequality machine*. Harcourt.

Teaching Online

Darby, F., & Lang, J. M. (2019). *Small teaching online: Applying learning science in online classes*. John Wiley & Sons.
Miller, M. D. (2014). *Minds online: Teaching effectively with technology*. Harvard University Press.
Nilson, L. B., & Goodson, L. A. (2017). *Online teaching at its best: Merging instructional design with teaching and learning research*. Jossey-Bass.
Stachowiak, B. (2020). *The productive online and offline professor: A practical guide*. Stylus.

Culturally Responsive and Inclusive Teaching

Chávez, A. F., & Longerbeam, S. D. (2016). *Teaching across cultural strengths: A guide to balancing integrated and individuated cultural frameworks in college teaching*. Stylus.
Hammond, Z. (2015). *Culturally Responsive Teaching and the Brain: Promoting Authentic Engagement and Rigor Among Culturally and Linguistically Diverse Students*. Corwin.
Paris, D., & Alim, S. (Eds.). (2017). *Culturally Sustaining Pedagogies*. Teachers College Press.
Posey, A., & Novak, K. (2020). *Unlearning: Changing your beliefs and your classroom with UDL*. CAST.
Sathy, V., & Hogan, K. (2019, July 22). *How to Make Your Teaching More Inclusive*. Retrieved July 11, 2020, from https://www.chronicle.com/interactives/20190719_inclusive_teaching
Tobin, T. J., & Behling, K. (2018). *Reach everyone, teach everyone: Universal Design for Learning in higher education*. West Virginia University Press.
Winkelmes, M.-A., Boye, A., & Tapp, S. (Eds.). (2019). *Transparent design in higher education teaching and leadership*. Stylus.

Discipline-Specific Teaching Resources

Gurung, R. A., Chick, N. L., & Haynie, A. (2009). *Exploring signature pedagogies: Approaches to teaching disciplinary habits of mind*. Stylus.
UNC-Charlotte's Center for Teaching and Learning hosts a list of discipline-specific journals on teaching. https://teaching.uncc.edu/learning-resources/sotl/sotl-journals#discipline-specific-journals

National Center for case study teaching in science. (n.d.). Retrieved July 12, 2020, from https://sciencecases.lib.buffalo.edu/

Grading

Feldman, J. (2019). Grading for equity: What it is, why it matters, and how it can transform schools and classrooms. Thousand Oaks, CA: Corwin.

Inoue, A. (n.d.). Home. Retrieved July 11, 2020, from https://wac.colostate.edu/books/perspectives/labor/

Nilson, L. B., & Stanny, C. J. (2014). *Specifications grading: Restoring rigor, motivating students, and saving faculty time*. Stylus.

Rubric Maker. (n.d.). Retrieved July 12, 2020, from https://rubric-maker.com/

Stommel, J. (2020, March 03). "How to Ungrade." Retrieved July 11, 2020, from https://www.jessestommel.com/how-to-ungrade/

Walvoord, B. E., Anderson, V. J., & Angelo, T. A. (1998). Effective grading: A tool for learning and assessment. Jossey-Bass.

Sample Teaching Statements

University of Michigan's Center for Research on Learning and Teaching: this webpage offers examples of teaching statements from many disciplines; visit https://crlt.umich.edu/tstrategies/tstpum

NOTES

NOTES TO CHAPTER 1

1. Maria is a pseudonym of a PhD interviewed by Aeron and Stephanie. We are using these interviewees' comments anonymously, but with their permission.
2. R1 is often used as shorthand for the Carnegie Classification that describes a doctoral granting institution with very high research activity. A Hispanic Serving Institution is a federal designation describing an institution with at least 25% or more of its full-time or full-time equivalent student enrollment self-reporting as Hispanic or Latino.
3. Since being boring is not one of Aeron's insecurities, she was able to approach the situation with curiosity instead of anger. After he woke up (unaware that he had been snoring), she asked him in a neutral tone to stay after class and then explained what had happened. He was immediately apologetic and explained that he worked as a bouncer until the early morning hours. He vowed to drink more coffee and the incident did not reoccur. Instead, Aeron developed a respect for the student's determination to succeed in the course despite his grueling schedule.
4. Christopher Caterine, in his recent book, *Leaving Academia*, estimates that "only about 1.2% of people who enter graduate programs in the arts and humanities earn a tenure-track position at a leading institution" (8).
5. According to The Hope Center for College, Community, and Justice's 2018 survey, 45% of college students surveyed were food insecure in the prior 30 days, 56% were housing insecure in the previous year, and 17% of respondents were homeless in the previous year (2019).

6. According to statistics collected by the Gates Foundation, 56% of college students are women; 45% are over 21; 44 identify as non-white; 36% receive Pell Grants; 26% work full time; 28% have children; 28 % take at least some online courses, and a growing number are veterans.
7. Chávez and Longerbeam argue for an approach they term "teaching across cultural strengths," which recognizes and values both *individuated* cultures, where learning tends to be more private, compartmentalized, linear, and contextually isolated; and *interdependent* cultural frameworks, where learning is generally more interconnected, mutual, reflective, cyclical, and contextually dependent. Chávez and Longerbeam are certainly not the first to point out that American universities are designed upon northern European educational models that are grounded in individuated, competitive cultural attitudes toward learning.
8. A theory of learning based on the work of Piaget and Vygotsky that argues that learning happens through direct experience and is connected to prior knowledge.

NOTES TO CHAPTER 2

1. You might even be in one of the several graduate programs that are currently thinking about their own design by re-examining the value of comprehensive exams, thesis or dissertation structures, and required coursework or internships. These design conversations arose specifically because graduate students told their programs that the original frameworks weren't preparing them for life after graduate school (Cassuto, 2015; Pettit, 2019).

NOTES TO CHAPTER 3

1. See Joshua Eyler's excellent summary in Chapter 2 of his book, *How Humans Learn*.
2. A certain amount of nervousness can help energize you, as Kelly McGonigal argues in *The Upside of Stress*.

NOTES TO CHAPTER 4

1. And while active learning may only be metaphorically lifesaving, it is definitely money saving for students. Out of 29,300 total students in the control condition (nonactive learning), the authors' research indicates that 3,516 more of

those students would have passed their course if it had been taught with active learning strategies, and those students could have avoided wasting an estimated $3,500,000 in tuition dollars on a failed course (Freeman et al., 2014, p. 8413).

2. See Chapter 3 of Jay Howard's *Discussion in the College Classroom* for a review of the research on who is more likely to become a dominant talker in the classroom, and the disparities between both instructor and student perceptions of participation and observable behavior.
3. There are many excellent recent books on learning science, such as *Make it Stick* and *How Learning Works*. Also useful is *Retrieval Practice*, the website of cognitive scientist, Pooja K. Agarwal.
4. There are some fascinating new books that discuss how learning works and how we can apply this research to the college classroom (see resources in the Appendix).

NOTES TO CHAPTER 6

1. For more examples of the UnEssay, see the professional websites of Marc Kissel (https://marckissel.netlify.app/post/on-the-unessay) or Cate Denial (https://catherinedenial.org/blog/uncategorized/the-unessay/).

REFERENCES

Agarwal, P. K. (n.d.). Interleaving: Boost learning by mixing it up—retrieval practice. Retrieved September 15, 2021, from https://www.retrievalpractice.org/interleaving

American Sociological Association. (2020, February 18). Reconsidering Student Evaluations of Teaching. Retrieved July 12, 2020, from https://www.asanet.org/press-center/press-releases/reconsidering-student-evaluations-teaching

Anderson, L. W., & Krathwohl, D. R. (2000). *A Taxonomy for Learning, Teaching, and Assessing: A Revision of Bloom's Taxonomy of Educational Objectives*. Longman.

Anft, M. (2018). Committed but concerned: How faculty view their work, their profession, and the leadership of colleges. *The Chronicle of Higher Education* [Research brief].

Angelo, T. A., & Cross, K. P. (1993). *Classroom assessment techniques: a handbook for college teachers*. Jossey-Bass.

Arday, J. (2018). Understanding mental health: What are the issues for Black and ethnic minority students at university? *Social Sciences*, 7(196), 1–25.

Attewell, P., Heil, S., & Reisel, L. (2012). What is academic momentum? And does it matter? *Education Evaluation and Policy Analysis*, *34*(1), 27–44.

Barnard College (n.d.) *Reacting to the Past*. Retrieved February 23, 2021, from https://reacting.barnard.edu/

Barreira, P., Basilico, M., & Bolotnyy, V. (n.d.). *Graduate student mental health: Lessons from American economics departments*. [Working paper].

Bauer, A. (2018, November 29). The two-sex system: Fact or fallacy? [STIRS student case study]. Retrieved July 7, 2020, from https://www.aacu.org/stirs/casestudies/bauer

Bean, J. (2011). *Engaging Ideas* (2nd ed.). Jossey-Bass.

Bettiner, E. P., Terry Long, B., & Taylor, E. S. (2016). When inputs are outputs: The case of graduate student instructors. *Economics of Education Review*, 52(June), 63–76.

Biggs, J. B. (1999). *Teaching for quality learning at university*. Society for Research into Higher Education : Open University Press.
Blagg, K., Whitmore Schanzenbach, D., Gundersen, C., & Ziliak, J. (2017). Assessing food insecurity on campus. Retrieved September 15, 2021, from http://www.urban.org/research/publication/assessing-food-insecurity-campus
Blaich, C., Pascarella, E. T., Roksa, J., & Wise, K. (2016). Instructional clarity and organization: It's not new or fancy, but it matters. *Change, 48*(4), 6-13.
Blum, S. (Ed.). (2020). *Ungrading: Why rating students undermines learning (and what to do instead)*. West Virginia University Press.
Boice, B. (1996). Classroom incivilities. *Research in Higher Education, 37*(4), 453–486. doi:10.1007/bf01730110
Bonwell, C. C., & Eison, J. A. (1991). *Active learning: Creating excitement in the classroom*. ASHE-ERIC Higher Education Reports.
Boyer, E. L. (1990). *Scholarship reconsidered*. The Carnegie Foundation for the Advancement of Teaching.
Brookfield, S. D. (2015). *The skillful teacher: On technique, trust, and responsiveness in the classroom*. John Wiley & Sons.
Brookfield, S. & Preskill, S. (1999). *Discussion as a way of teaching*. Jossey-Bass.
Brown, P. C., Roediger, H. L., III, & McDaniel, M. A. (2014). *Make it stick: The science of successful learning*. Belknap Press.
Burleson, M. H., Trevathan, W. R., & Todd, M. (2006). In the mood for love or vice versa? Exploring the relations among sexual activity, physical affection, affect, and stress in the daily lives of mid-aged women. *Archives of Sexual Behavior, 36*(3), 357–368. doi:10.1007/s10508-006-9071-1
Butler, R. (1988). Enhancing and undermining intrinsic motivation: the effects of task-involving and ego-involving evaluation on interest and performance. *Br J Educ Psychol. 58*,(1), 1–14.
Butrymowicz, S. (2017). Most colleges enroll many students who aren't prepared for higher education. Retrieved September 14, 2021, from http://hechingerreport.org/colleges-enroll-students-arent-prepared-higher-education/
Calder, L. (2006). Uncoverage: Toward a signature pedagogy for the history survey. *Journal of American History, 92*(4), 1358–1370. doi:10.2307/4485896
Canning, E., Muenks, K., Green, D., Murphy, M., Drake, S. (2019). STEM faculty who believe ability is fixed have larger racial achievement gaps and inspire less student motivation in their classes. *Science Advances* 5(2), eaau4734. DOI: 10.1126/sciadv.aau4734
Carlyle, T. (1897). *Sartor resartus*. G.P. Putnam's Sons.
Cassuto, L. (2015). *The graduate school mess*. Harvard University Press.
Caterine, C. L. (2020). *Leaving academia: A practical guide*. Princeton University Press.

Cavanagh, S. R. (2016). *The spark of learning: Energizing the college classroom with the science of emotion*. West Virginia University Press.

Chambliss, D. & Takacs, C. (2014). *How college works*. Harvard University Press.

Chávez, A. F., & Longerbeam, S. D. (2016). *Teaching across cultural strengths: A guide to balancing integrated and individuated cultural frameworks in college teaching*. Stylus.

Chen, Y.-W. (2014). "Are You an Immigrant?": Identity-Based Critical Reflections of Teaching Intercultural Communication. *New Directions for Teaching and Learning, 2014*(138), 5–16. https://doi.org/10.1002/tl.20092

Chick, N. (n.d.). Metacognition. *Vanderbilt Center for Teaching Guide*. Retrieved February 1, 2021, from https://cft.vanderbilt.edu/guides-sub-pages/metacognition/

Chickering, A., & Gamson, Z. (1987). Seven principles for good practice in undergraduate education. American Association for Higher Education Bulletin. March 1987, 3–7.

Clance, P. R., & Imes, S. A. (1978). The imposter phenomenon in high achieving women: Dynamics and therapeutic intervention. *Psychotherapy: Theory, Research & Practice, 15*(3), 241–247. doi:10.1037/h0086006

Cooper, M. (1995). Cooperative Learning: An Approach for Large Enrollment Courses. Journal of Chemical Education 72 (2), 162.

Creasman, C. (2016). American History 2020 [course syllabus]. http://frontdoor.valenciacollege.edu/materials.cfm?uid=ccreasman

Counseling Services. (n.d.). Retrieved September 18, 2021, from https://counseling.uoregon.edu/disruptive-and-threatening-students

Croizet, J., & Claire, T. (1998). Extending the concept of stereotype threat to social class: The intellectual underperformance of students from low socioeconomic backgrounds. *Personality and Social Psychology Bulletin, 24*(6), 588–594.

Currier, D. (2020). Sociology 1114: Contemporary U.S. Society [course syllabus]. https://www.randolphcollege.edu/online/wpcontent/uploads/sites/102/2020/05/SOC_114_syllabus.pdf

Dalai Lama [Tenzin Gyatso], Tutu, D., & Abrams, D. (2016). *The book of joy. Lasting happiness in a changing world*. Avery.

Danish, J. (2012, May). Helping students use theory to see the world differently. Retrieved September 15, 2021, from https://citl.indiana.edu/teaching-resources/faculty-spotlights/joshua-danish.html

Darby, F., & Lang, J. M. (2019). *Small teaching online: Applying learning science in online classes*. Jossey-Bass.

Davidson, C. (2017). *The new education*. Hatchett.

Delta College (n.d.) *Course Outcomes and Objectives: A Survey of Later Western Civilization (Delta College)* American Historical Association. https://www.historians.org/teaching-and-learning/teaching-resources-for-historians/resources-for-tuning-the-history-discipline/two-year/community-colleges/course-outcomes-and-objectives-a-survey-of-later-western-civilization-(delta-college)

Denial, C. (2019, April 26). The UnEssay. Retrieved February 23, 2021, from https://catherinedenial.org/blog/uncategorized/the-unessay/

Deslauriers, L., McCarty, L. S., Miller, K., Callaghan, K., & Kestin, G. (2019). Measuring actual learning versus feeling of learning in response to being actively engaged in the classroom. *PNAS, 116*(39), 19251–19257.

Drake, S., Auletto, A., & Cowen, J. M. (2019). Grading teachers: Race and gender differences in low evaluation ratings and teacher employment outcomes: *American Educational Research Journal*. 56(5), 1800 – 1833.

Driscoll, A., & Wood, S. (2007). Developing outcomes-based assessment for learner-centered education: A faculty introduction. Sterling, VA: Stylus.

Dubey, P., & Geanakoplos, J. (2010). Grading exams. *Games and Economic Behavior.* 69(1), 72–94.

Dubson, M. (n.d.). *PHYS 1110 General Physics 1.* [Course syllabus]. https://canvas.colorado.edu/courses/54209/assignments/syllabus

Duffy, M., Thanhouser, C., & Derry, H. (2019, June 24). A lack of evidence for six times more anxiety and depression in US graduate students than in the general population. Retrieved July 4, 2020, from https://www.nature.com/articles/s41587-019-0179-y

Dweck, C. S. (2016). *Mindset: The new psychology of success* (Updated). Ballantine.

Eddy, S. L., & Hogan, K. A. (2014). Getting under the hood: How and for whom does increasing course structure work? *CBE—Life Sciences Education, 13*(3), 453–468. doi:10.1187/cbe.14-03-0050

Eells, W. (1930). Reliability of repeated grading of essay type examinations. *Journal of Educational Psychology* 21 (1), 48-52.

Elder, C. L. & Champine, K. (2016, December 26). Designing high-impact "writing-to-learn" math assignments for killer courses. [Special issue on WAC and high-impact practices]. *Across the Disciplines*, 13(4). Retrieved September 15, 2021, from https://wac.colostate.edu/docs/atd/hip/elder_champine2016.pdf

El-Ghoroury, N. H., Galper, D. I., Sawaqdeh, A., & Bufka, L. F. (2012). Stress, coping, and barriers to wellness among psychology graduate students. *Training and Education in Professional Psychology, 6*(2), 122–134. https://doi.org/10.1037/a0028768

Ellenbogen, J. M., Payne, J. D., & Stickgold, R. (2006). The role of sleep in declarative memory consolidation: Passive, permissive, active or none? *Current Opinion in Neurobiology*, *16*(6), 716–722.

Esarey, J., & Valdes, N. (2020). Unbiased, reliable, and valid student evaluations can still be unfair. *Assessment & Evaluation in Higher Education,* 45:8, 1–15. doi:10.1080/02602938.2020.1724875

Evans, T., Bira, L., Gastelum, J., Todd Weiss, & L., Vanderford, N. (2018). Evidence for a mental health crisis in graduate education. *Nat Biotechnol* 36, 282–284. https://doi-org.libproxy.unm.edu/10.1038/nbt.4089

Eyler, J. R. (2018). *How humans learn: The science and stories behind effective college teaching*. West Virginia University Press.

Feldman, J. (2018). *Grading for equity. What it is, why it matters, and how it can transform schools and classrooms*. Corwin.

Fink, L. D. (2013). *Creating significant learning experiences: An integrated approach to designing college courses*. Jossey-Bass.

Frederick, P. (1982). The dreaded discussion: Ten ways to start. *To Improve the Academy*, *10*, 205–215.

Freeman, S., Eddy, S. L., McDonough, M., Smith, M. K., Nnadozie, O., Jordt, H., & Wenderoth, M. P. (2014). Active learning increases student performance in science, engineering, and mathematics. *PNAS*, *111*(23), 8410–8415.

Gallup. (2014). *The 2014 Gallup-Purdue index report: A study of more than 30,000 college graduates across the U.S.* https://www.gallup.com/services/176768/2014-gallup-purdue-index-report.aspx

Gannon, K. (2019, September 2). Teaching online will make you a better teacher in any setting. *The Chronicle of Higher Education*. www.chronicle.com

Gannon, K. (2020). *Radical hope: A teaching manifesto*. West Virginia University Press.

Gardiner, M., & Aurora, V. (2013). Impostor syndrome-proof yourself and your community. Usenix. Retrieved July 4, 2020, from https://www.usenix.org/blog/impostor-syndrome-proof-yourself-and-your-community

Gay, G. (2000). *Culturally responsive teaching: Theory, research. & practice*. Teachers College.

Ginsberg, M., & Wlodkowski, R. (2015) *Diversity and motivation: Culturally responsive teaching in college*. Jossey-Bass.

Goldrick-Rab, S. (2016). *Paying the price: College costs, financial aid, and the betrayal of the American dream*. University of Chicago Press.

Goldrick-Rab, S., Richardson, J., Schneider, J., Hernandez, A., & Cady, C. (2018, May). Still hungry and homeless in college. Retrieved July 6, 2020, from https://www.theotx.org/wp-content/uploads/2018/05/Wisconsin-HOPE-Lab-Still-Hungry-and-Homeless.pdf

Gonzalez, J. (2015). Icebreakers that rock. *Cult of Pedagogy*. Retrieved July 21, 2020, from https://www.cultofpedagogy.com/classroom-icebreakers/

Gooblar, D. (2018, April 03). 4 Ideas for avoiding faculty burnout. Retrieved July 4, 2020, from https://www.chronicle.com/article/4-Ideas-for-Avoiding-Faculty/243010

Gooblar, D. (2019). *The missing course*. Harvard University Press.

Good, C., Aronson, J., & Harder, J. A. (2008). Problems in the pipeline: Stereotype threat and women's achievement in high-level math courses. *Journal of Applied Developmental Psychology*, *29*(1), 17–28. doi:10.1016/j.appdev.2007.10.004

Gross-Loh, C. (2016, December 16). How praise became a consolation prize: Helping children confront challenges requires a more nuanced understanding of the "growth mindset." *The Atlantic*. Retrieved September 11, 2021, from https://www.theatlantic.com/education/archive/2016/12/how-praise-became-a-consolation-prize/510845/

Haak, D. C., HilleRisLambers, J., Pitre, E., & Freeman, S. (2011). Increased structure and active learning reduce the achievement gap in introductory biology. *Science*, *332*(6034), 1213–1216.

Hammond, Z. (2015). *Culturally responsive teaching and the brain: Promoting authentic engagement and rigor among culturally and linguistically diverse students*. Corwin.

Handelsman, M. M., Briggs, W. L., Sullivan, N., & Towler, A. (2005). A measure of college student course engagement. *The Journal of Educational Research, 98*(3), 184–192. doi:10.3200/joer.98.3.184-192

Haswell, R. H. (1983). Minimal marking. *College English, 45*(6), 600–604.

Hebbani, A., & Hendrix, K. G. (2014). Capturing the Experiences of International Teaching Assistants in the US American Classroom. *New Directions for Teaching and Learning, 2014*(138), 61–72. https://doi.org/10.1002/tl.20097

Hodges, C., Moore, S., Lockee, B., Trust, T., & Bond, A. (2020). The difference between emergency remote teaching and online learning. *Educause Review*. Retrieved September 25, 2021, from https://er.educause.edu/articles/2020/3/the-difference-between-emergency-remote-teaching-and-online-learning

Holman, M., Key, E., & Kreitzer, R. (2019). Evidence of bias in standard evaluations of teaching. Retrieved July 11, 2020, from https://docs.google.com/document/d/14JiF-fT--F3Qaefjv2jMRFRWUS8TaaT9JjbYke1fgxE/edit

Hope Center for College, Community, and Justice. (2019, April 30). College and university basic needs insecurity: A national #RealCollege survey report. Retrieved December 30, 2020, from https://hope4college.com/college-and-university-basic-needs-insecurity-a-national-realcollege-survey-report/

Howard, J. (2015). *Discussion in the college classroom: Getting your students engaged and participating in person and online*. Jossey-Bass.

Humphreys, B., Johnson, R.T., & Johnson, D.W. (1982). Effects of cooperative, competitive, and individualistic learning on students' achievement in science class. *J Res Sci Teach*. *19*(5), 351–356.

Huston, T. (2009). *Teaching what you don't know*. Harvard University Press.

Inoue, A. (2019) Labor-based grading contracts: Building equity and inclusion in the compassionate writing classroom. University Press of Colorado. https://wac.colostate.edu/books/perspectives/labor/

Institute of International Education. (2020). "International Students by Academic Level, 1999/00 – 20219/20." *Open Doors Report on International Educational Exchange*. Retrieved from http://www.opendoorsdata.org

Jack, A. A. (2019, September 10). I was a low-income college student. Classes weren't the hard part. Retrieved July 6, 2020, from https://www.nytimes.com/interactive/2019/09/10/magazine/college-inequality

Janasz, S. C., & Sullivan, S. E. (2004). Multiple mentoring in academe: Developing the professorial network. *Journal of Vocational Behavior, 64*(2), 263–283. doi:10.1016/j.jvb.2002.07.001

Jenkins, D., & Bailey, T. (2017). *Early momentum metrics: Why they matter for college improvement* [Community College Research Center research brief No. 65]. Columbia University.

Kang, J. F. (n.d.). Data tables. Retrieved February 14, 2021, from https://ncses.nsf.gov/pubs/nsf21308/data-tables

Kaplan, M., O'Neal, C., Meizlish, D., Carillo, R., & Kardia, D. Rubrics for evaluating statements of teaching philosophy. Retrieved September 15, 2021, from https://fora.aa.ufl.edu/docs/1//10Oct17//Biomedical_Educator_Rubric.pdf

Kissel, M. (2018, May 07). The UnEssay. Retrieved February 23, 2021, from https://marckissel.netlify.app/post/on-the-unessay/

Kohn, A. (2013). The case against grades. *Educational Leadership, 451*, 143–153. Retrieved July 7, 2020, from www.jstor.org/stable/42982088

Kurzweil, M., & Wyner, J. (2020, June 16). Rich kids are eating up the financial aid pot. Retrieved June 20, 2020, from https://www.nytimes.com/2020/06/16/opinion/coronavirus-college-rich-kids.html

Lackritz, J.R. (2004). Exploring burnout among university faculty: Incidence, performance and demographic issues. *Teaching & Teacher Education, 20*(7), 713–729.

Ladson-Billings, G. (1995). Toward a theory of culturally relevant pedagogy. *American Research Journal, 32*(3), 465–491.

Lai, J. S., Hiles, S., Bisquera, A., Hure, A. J., McEvoy, M., & Attia, J. (2013). A systematic review and meta-analysis of dietary patterns and depression in community-dwelling adults. *The American Journal of Clinical Nutrition, 99*(1), 181–197. https://doi.org/10.3945/ajcn.113.069880

Lang, J. M. (2008). *On course: A week-by-week guide to your first semester of college teaching*. Harvard University Press.

Lang, J. M. (2019, January 04). How to teach a good first day of class. Retrieved January 1, 2020, from https://www.chronicle.com/interactives/advice-firstday

Lieberman, C. (2019, March 25). Why you procrastinate (it has nothing to do with self-control). Retrieved July 6, 2020, from, https://www.nytimes.com/2019/03/25/smarter-living/why-you-procrastinate-it-has-nothing-to-do-with-self-control.html

Love, P. G. (1998). Cultural barriers facing lesbian, gay, and bisexual students at a catholic college. *Journal of Higher Education, 69*(3), 298–323.

Luna, Y. (2018). *SOC101: Introduction to sociology: Syllabus of practice.*

Retrieved February 17, 2021, from https://in.nau.edu/wp-content/uploads/sites/20/2019/02/SOC101-SYLLABUS-of-PRACTICE.pdf
Major, C. H. (2015). *Teaching online: A guide to theory, research, and practice.* Johns Hopkins University Press.
Marcus, J. (2019). 10 years later, goal of getting more Americans through college is way behind schedule. *The Hechinger Report.*
McFarland, J., Hussar, B., Wang, X., Zhang, J., Wang, K., Rathbun, A., Barmer, A., Forrest Cataldi, E., and Bullock Mann, F. (2018). The Condition of Education 2018 (NCES 2018-144). U.S. Department of Education. Washington, DC: National Center for Education Statistics. Retrieved September 12, 2021, from https://nces.ed.gov/pubsearch/pubsinfo. asp?pubid=2018144.
McGonigal, K. (2016). *The upside of stress: Why stress is good for you, and how to get good at it.* Avery.
McLaren, P. (2002). Critical pedagogy: A look at the major concepts. In A. Darder, R. D. Torres, & M. Baltodano (Eds.), The critical pedagogy reader (pp. 69–96). Routledge.
Meizlish, D., & Kaplan, M. (2008). Valuing and evaluating teaching in academic hiring: A multidisciplinary, cross-institutional study. *The Journal of Higher Education, 79*(5), 489–512. doi:10.1353/jhe.0.0017
Michigan Center for Research on Learning and Teaching (n.d.). Guidelines For Classroom Interactions. Retrieved July 6, 2020, from, http://crlt.umich.edu/examples-discussion-guidelines
Miller, M. D. (2014). *Minds online: Teaching effectively with technology.* Harvard University Press.
Miller, S., Kennedy, C., DeVoe, D., Hickey, M., Nelson, T., & Kogan, L. (2009). An examination of changes in oxytocin levels in men and women before and after interaction with a bonded dog. Anthrozoös, *22*(1), 31–42.
Nagoski, D. A., & Nagoski, P. E. (2019). *Burnout: The secret to unlocking the stress cycle.* Ballantine Books.
NCES Fast Facts (National Center for Education Statistics). (n.d.). Retrieved July 4, 2020, from https://nces.ed.gov/fastfacts/display.asp?id=61
Nelson, C. (2010). Dysfunctional illusions of rigor: Lessons from the scholarship of teaching and learning. *To Improve the Academy, 28*(1), 177–192. https://doi.org/10.1002/j.2334-4822.2010.tb00602.x
Nettles, K. D., Balogun, O. M., & Myers, L. W. (2003). A Broken Silence: Voices of African American Women in the Academy. *Contemporary Sociology, 32*(1), 107. doi:10.2307/3089882
Nevid, J. S., Pastva, A., & Mcclelland, N. (2012). Writing-to-learn assignments in introductory psychology. *Teaching of Psychology, 39*(4), 272–275. doi:10.1177/0098628312456622
New College of Florida. (n.d.). *Academics at New College.* Retrieved June 30, 2020, from https://www.ncf.edu/academics/academics-at-new-college/
Nilson, L. B. (2016, January 19). New ways to grade more effectively.

Inside Higher Ed. Retrieved August 20, 2018, from https://www.insidehighered.com/views/2016/01/19/new-ways-grade-more-effectively-essay

Omar, A. (2012, January). The power of storytelling to engage students. Retrieved September 25, 2021, from https://citl.indiana.edu/teaching-resources/faculty-spotlights/alwiya-omar.html

Parker, P. (2018). *The art of gathering: How we meet and why it matters*. Riverhead Books.

Patel, V. (2017, July 30). Training graduate students to be effective teachers. Retrieved July 10, 2018, from https://www.chronicle.com/article/Training-Graduate-Students-to/240783

Patterson-Stephens, S. M., Lane, T. B., & Vital, L. M. (2017). Black doctoral women: Exploring barriers and facilitators of success in graduate education. *Higher Education Politics & Economics, 3*(1), 157–180. doi:10.32674/hepe.v3i1.15

Patterson, T. E. (2016). Why do so many graduate students quit? Universities themselves may be contributing to burnout. *The Atlantic*. https://www.theatlantic.com/education/archive/2016/07/why-do-so-many-graduate-students-quit/490094/

Pekrun, R. (2006). The control-value theory of achievement emotions: Assumptions, corollaries, and implications for educational research and practice. *Educ Psychol Rev 18*, 315–341. https://doi.org/10.1007/s10648-006-9029-9

Pettit, E. (2019, August 21). Columbia Had Little Success Placing English Ph.D.s on the Tenure Track. "Alarm" Followed, and the University Responded. *The Chronicle of Higher Education*. www.chronicle.com

Race, P., & Pickford, R. (2007). *Making teaching work: Teaching smarter in post-compulsory education*. SAGE.

Revuluri, S. (2018, October 04). How to overcome impostor syndrome. Retrieved July 4, 2020, from https://www.chronicle.com/article/How-to-Overcome-Impostor/244700

Rhys, R. (n.d.). Stereotype: an overview. Retrieved July 6, 2020, from https://diversity.arizona.edu/sites/default/files/stereotype_threat_overview.pdf

Richmond, A. S., Boysen, G. A., & Gurung, R. A. R. (2016). *An evidence-based guide to college and university teaching: Developing the model teacher*. Routledge.

Rockquemore, K. (2011, October 3). Don't talk about mentoring. Retrieved July 4, 2020, from https://www.insidehighered.com/advice/2011/10/03/dont-talk-about-mentoring

Rockquermore, K. Laszloffy, T. (2008) *The Black academic's guide to winning tenure without losing your soul.* Lynne Rienner.

Sakulku, J. (2011). The impostor phenomenon. *International Journal of Behavioral Science*, *6*(1), 75–97.

Sanchez, S. (2019). Graduate climate survey of UNM. Unpublished.

Sarris, J., Logan, A. C., Akbaraly, T. N., Amminger, G. P., Balanzá-Martínez, V., Freeman, M. P., . . . Jacka, F. N. (2015). Nutritional medicine as mainstream in psychiatry. *The Lancet Psychiatry, 2*(3), 271–274. doi:10.1016/s2215-0366(14)00051-0

Schinske, J., & Tanner, K. (2014). Teaching more by grading less (or differently). *CBE—Life Sciences Education, 13*(2), 159–166. doi:10.1187/cbe.cbe-14-03-0054

Schippers, M., Scheepers, A. & Peterson, J. (2015). A scalable goal-setting intervention closes both the gender and ethnic minority achievement gap. *Palgrave Communications* 1, 15014. https://doi.org/10.1057/palcomms.2015.14

Schmader, T., & Johns, M. (2003). Converging evidence that stereotype threat reduces working memory capacity. *Journal of Personality and Social Psychology, 85*(3), 440–452. doi:10.1037/0022-3514.85.3.440

Seaman, J., Allen, I. E., & Seaman, J. (2018). *Grade Increase: Tracking Distance Education in the United States*. Babson Survey Research Group. https://www.bayviewanalytics.com/reports/gradeincrease.pdf

Shorr, A. (2017, July 17). Grad school is hard on mental health. Here's an antidote. Retrieved July 4, 2020, from https://www.chronicle.com/article/Grad-School-Is-Hard-on-Mental/240626

Shortlidge, E. E., & Eddy, S. L. (2018, June 25). The trade-off between graduate student research and teaching: A myth? Retrieved June 30, 2018, from https://journals.plos.org/plosone/article?id=10.1371/journal.pone.0199576

Sipress, J and Voelker, D. (2009). From learning history to doing history. *Exploring signature pedagogies: Approaches to teaching disciplinary habits* (R. A. R. Gurung, N. L. Chick, & A. Haynie, Eds.). (pp. 19–35), Stylus.

Showalter, E. (2002). *Teaching literature*. Wiley-Blackwell.

Smith, M. K., Wenderoth, M. P., & Tyler, M. (2013). The teaching demonstration: What faculty expect and how to prepare for this aspect of the job interview. *CBE—Life Sciences Education, 12*(1), 12–18. doi:10.1187/cbe.12-09-0161

Smith, R. M. (2014). *Conquering the content: A blueprint for online course design and development* (2nd ed.). Jossey-Bass.

Sorcinelli, M. D., & Yun, J. (2007). From mentor to mentoring networks: Mentoring in the new academy. *Change: The Magazine of Higher Learning, 39*(6), 58–61. doi:10.3200/chng.39.6.58-c4

Southern New Hampshire University (n.d.). *General Education Learning Goals and Outcomes, (Southern New Hampshire University)* American Historical Association. https://www.historians.org/teaching-and-learning/teaching-resources-for-historians/resources-for-tuning-the-history-discipline/four-year-private-universities/general-education-learning-goals-and-outcomes-southern-hew-hampshire-university

Spencer, S. J., Steele, C. M., & Quinn, D. M. (1999). Stereotype threat and women's math performance. *Journal of Experimental Social Psychology, 35*(1), 4–28. doi:10.1006/jesp.1998.1373

Stark, P., Ottoboni, K., & Boring, A. (2016, Jan. 7). Student evaluations of teaching (mostly) do not measure teaching effectiveness. *ScienceOpen Research*. doi:10.14293/s2199-1006.1.sor-edu.aetbzc.v1

Steele, C. M., & Aronson, J. (1995). Stereotype threat and the intellectual test performance of African Americans. *Journal of Personality and Social Psychology, 69(5)*, 797–811.

Stommel, J. (2018, May 04). Why I don't grade. Retrieved August 20, 2018, from https://www.jessestommel.com/why-i-dont-grade/

Subtirelu, N. C. (2015). She does have an accent but...: Race and language ideology in students' evaluations of mathematics instructors on RateMyProfessors.com. *Language in Society, 44*(1), 35–62. doi:10.1017/s0047404514000736

Supiano, B. (2019). Grades can hinder learning. What should professors use instead? *The Chronicle of Higher Education*. Retrieved Jan 10, 2020, from https://www.chronicle.com/interactives/20190719_ungrading

Supiano, B. (2018, April 14). How colleges can cultivate students' sense of belonging. *The Chronicle of Higher Education*. www.chronicle.com

Taylor, S. E., Klein, L. C., Lewis, B. P., Gruenewald, T. L., Gurung, R. A., & Updegraff, J. A. (2000). Biobehavioral responses to stress in females: Tend-and-befriend, not fight-or-flight. *Psychological Review, 107*(3), 411–429. doi:10.1037/0033-295x.107.3.411

Tierney, J. (2013) Why teachers secretly hate grading. *The Atlantic*. https://www.theatlantic.com/national/archive/2013/01/why-teachers-secretly-hate-grading-papers/266931/

Tuitt, F. (2011). Black Like Me. *Journal of Black Studies, 43*(2), 186-206. doi:10.1177/0021934711413271

Ubell, R. (2017). *Going online: Perspectives on digital learning*. Routledge.

UC Davis Graduate School of Management. (2018, April 20). 5 tips for grad school stress. Retrieved July 4, 2020, from https://gsm.ucdavis.edu/blog/5-tips-grad-school-stress

University of Oregon Counseling Services. (n.d.). *Disruptive and threatening students*. https://counseling.uoregon.edu/disruptive-and-threatening-students

van der Helm, E., & Walker, M. P. (2009). Overnight therapy? The role of sleep in emotional brain processing. *Psychology Bulletin, 135*(5), 731–748.

Vargas, L. (2002). Women faculty of color in the white classroom narratives on the pedagogical implications of teacher diversity. New York: Lang.

Verschelden, C. (2017). *Bandwidth recovery: Helping students reclaim cognitive resources lost to poverty, racism, and social marginalization*. Stylus.

Vygotsky, L. (1980). Mind in society: Development of higher psychological processes. M. Cole, V. John-Steiner, S. Scribner, & E. Souberman (Eds.). Harvard University Press.

Walton, G., & G. Cohen. (2011). A brief social-belonging intervention improves academic and health outcomes of minority students. *Science, 331*(6023), 1447–1451.

Watson, N. F., Badr, M. S., Belenky, G., Bliwise, D. L., Buxton, O. M., Buysse, D., Dinges, D. F., Gangwisch, J., Grandner, M. A., Kushida, C., Malhotra, R. K., Martin, J. L., Patel, S. R., Quan, S. F., Tasali, E., Twery, M., Croft, J. B., Maher, E., Barrett, J. A., ... Heald, J. L. (n.d.). Joint consensus statement of the American Academy of Sleep Medicine and Sleep Research Society on the recommended amount of sleep for a healthy adult: Methodology and discussion. *SLEEP*, *38*(8), 1161–1183.

Watts, J. & Robertson, N. (2011). Burnout in university teaching staff: a systematic literature review, *Educational Research*, *53*(1), 33–50, DOI: 10.1080/00131881.2011.552235

Wiggins, G., & McTighe, J. (2005). *Understanding by Design*. Association for Supervision and Curriculum Development.

Wilkinson, R. G., & Pickett, K. (2009). *The spirit level: Why more equal societies almost always do better*. Allen Lane.

Wineburg, S. (1999). "Historical Thinking and Other Unnatural Acts." The Phi Delta Kappan 80 (3), 488–499.

Wood, L. M. (2020, January 26). Participate in a new survey on Ph.D. mental health. Retrieved July 4, 2020, from https://www.chronicle.com/article/Participate-in-a-New-Survey-on/247899

Wright, C. (2016). I am a Marine. *Pedagogy*, *16*(3), 517–525.

Yeager, D. S., Purdie-Vaughns, V., Garcia, J., Apfel, N., Brzustoski, P., Master, A., Hessert, W. T., & Williams, M. E. (2013). Breaking the cycle of mistrust: Wise interventions to provide critical feedback across the racial divide. *Journal of Experimental Psychology: General, 143(2),* 804–824.

Yeager, D. S., Hanselman, P., Walton, G. M., Murray, J. S., Crosnoe, R., Muller, C., . . . Dweck, C. S. (2019). A national experiment reveals where a growth mindset improves achievement. *Nature, 573*(7774), 364–369. doi:10.1038/s41586-019-1466-y

Yesko, J. (2014). Higher ed should create an alternative to ABD status. *Inside Higher Ed*. https://www.insidehighered.com/advice/2014/07/25/higher-ed-should-create-alternative-abd-status-essay

INDEX

TEACHING AND LEARNING IN HIGHER EDUCATION

Remembering and Forgetting in the Age of Technology: Teaching, Learning, and the Science of Memory in a Wired World
Michelle D. Miller

Skim, Dive, Surface: Teaching Digital Reading
Jenae Cohn

Minding Bodies: How Physical Space, Sensation, and Movement Affect Learning
Susan Hrach

Ungrading: Why Rating Students Undermines Learning (and What to Do Instead)
Edited by Susan D. Blum

Radical Hope: A Teaching Manifesto
Kevin M. Gannon

Teaching about Race and Racism in the College Classroom: Notes from a White Professor
Cyndi Kernahan

Intentional Tech: Principles to Guide the Use of Educational Technology in College Teaching
Derek Bruff

Geeky Pedagogy: A Guide for Intellectuals, Introverts, and Nerds Who Want to Be Effective Teachers
Jessamyn Neuhaus

How Humans Learn: The Science and Stories behind Effective College Teaching
Joshua R. Eyler

Reach Everyone, Teach Everyone: Universal Design for Learning in Higher Education
Thomas J. Tobin and Kirsten T. Behling

Teaching the Literature Survey Course: New Strategies for College Faculty
Gwynn Dujardin, James M. Lang, and John A. Staunton

The Spark of Learning: Energizing the College Classroom with the Science of Emotion
Sarah Rose Cavanagh